W9-CMB-714

Three Days

Three Days

A MOTHER'S STORY

MELODY CARLSON

DOUBLEDAY LARGE PRINT HOME LIBRARY EDITION

Revell

Grand Rapids, Michigan

This Large Print Edition, prepared especially for Doubleday Large Print Home Library, contains the complete, unabridged text of the original Publisher's Edition.

Published by Fleming H. Revell
a division of Baker Publishing Group
P.O. Box 6287, Grand Rapids, MI 49516-6287

Printed in the United States of America

ISBN 0-7394-5087-5

All Scripture is the author's paraphrase.

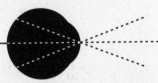

This Large Print Book carries the
Seal of Approval of N.A.V.H.

Dedicated to my "Joseph"

And there were many other things that Jesus did, but even if they were written out, one story at a time, I do not think the entire world could possibly contain all those books. Amen.

John 21:25

Preface

First of all, you must understand that this book is a work of fiction. And, although I have attempted to do my research, I am neither theologian nor historian. I am simply a storyteller who asked the question, What is the rest of Mary's story?

Just as I was beginning this project, a friend said, "What makes you think you can write about the mother of Jesus?" And I had to agree with her that it did seem quite an undertaking, but I felt driven to try. Now that I am finished, I can say it is probably the most spiritually fulfilling book I have ever written. Yet I still feel a need to explain what qualified me to write Mary's story (not that I feel qualified).

For starters, consider the numbers. While writing this book, I was almost exactly the same age as Mary when she stood at the foot of the cross (I won't give you that number, but historians estimate she was around fifteen when she gave birth to Jesus). And, like Mary at that same time, I have known the Lord for thirty-three years. I will admit I am not really a numbers person, but these figures got my attention.

I am also the mother of grown sons, and I too have experienced the pain of, not completely but very nearly, losing an adult son (that is another story). And I have suffered a mother's midnight heartache when she does not know where her son is or if he is all right. I have also felt the pain of parenting an unbelieving child. You did not know that Mary had unbelieving children? See, there is much to learn.

So please forgive me if I have not gotten it completely right or if my imagination does not match what you believe may have happened. Most of all, I hope that you can enjoy the spirit of this tale as you take a creative journey with me, and I hope even more that you'll feel closer to our Lord and Savior when you are finished.

—Melody Carlson

1

In the same way that I grind barley into flour, Jehovah's fist has ground my heart into dust today, and I fear the slightest breath of doubt could blow it all away. And so I must contain my emotions and focus on something beyond the ugliness I have witnessed during these past twelve hours. I must find something to distract my mind from the brutal images of my son's torture and execution—images, I am sure, that will accompany me throughout the rest of my earthly days.

I have heard that the events of a lifetime can flash past the mind's eye in the moments that precede death. I do not personally know this to be true (since I am still alive, albeit barely), but as I sit here in the darkness, knowing I will never find sleep, I find there is comfort in remembering. And so I will go back to a time and place that is happier.

My earliest memories are rooted in a garden. As a small child I trailed behind my mother whenever she went to the family garden, and there I was content to simply sit and dig in the dirt, using a broken shard of pottery for my spade. The damp, musky smell of the earth has always been a pure tonic to me. And the cool sensation of moist soil beneath my feet never fails to invigorate my soul. I believe a garden is God's promise that life will continue.

As I grew older I learned to distinguish weeds from seedlings, and how to transplant and even graft. I knew the best time to harvest, and, perhaps even more importantly, I knew how to gather and save seeds for the next planting. For this is how the circle of life continues.

Working in the garden was never a chore for me. Nothing felt better than being out there, barefooted and with sleeves pushed up, tending my herbs, beans, cucumbers . . . celebrating the freshness of a new day. I am sure I believed that all the secrets of the world could be contained in a single garden, because that is where I came to understand so much about life and love and truth. And that is where I felt closest to the Lord God Jehovah. To me, the garden was a true place of worship.

And for that reason I suppose it is not so very surprising that the angel of God would go looking for me there. Not that I ever expected the angel of God to seek out my humble presence. Far from it! In fact, I was only a young girl at the time— and not an outstanding one, at that. My family was among the least impressive of Nazareth, quiet, hardworking people who were usually overlooked by anyone of influence.

To this day I have no doubt there were plenty of other girls in my village who seemed more suitable for the promise that was laid before me. There were prettier ones, smarter ones, and most assuredly there were many from families more prominent than mine. I am sure old men in my hometown still scratch their beards and wonder why their quiet and insignificant little Mary should be chosen for such an awesome responsibility—that is, unless they are part of the group who still doubt that God chose me at all. But I know in my heart what is true. And I know that God's ways are mysterious and many difficult questions languish and then perish for lack of answers.

Not that I did not question these things for myself back then. Who would not? I had recently been promised in marriage to a friend of the family—a good man by the name of Joseph. That alone had been surprising enough. I could not even imagine how a respected man like Joseph the carpenter should be interested in someone like me, but I must admit to being flattered by his attention. Still, I am sure that the actual thought of marriage and all that it stood for seemed far away and removed at the time.

So you can imagine my complete surprise when an angel appeared to me in the garden, announcing that I was to be blessed among women and that I had found favor with the Lord. Stunned at what I knew to be an unearthly presence, I dropped my basket of freshly picked figs and fell to my knees. I still remember looking down at my trembling hands, noticing the dark lines of garden dirt beneath my fingernails as I waited for the angel to continue.

This magnificent being told me not to be frightened by his greeting. As if that were even possible! And then he announced that I, Mary of Nazareth, would carry in my womb and give birth to God's own Son—the very Son of the Lord God Jehovah. It was good that I was not a fainter.

"He will be great," the angel continued. "He will be called the Son of the highest, and the Lord God will give him the throne of David, and his kingdom will reign forever and ever."

Naturally, I was still trying to figure out how I could possibly carry God's baby in my womb. I may have been young and inexperienced, but I knew enough about the ways of life to realize that a woman must be intimate with a man to bear a child.

And so I boldly asked the angel how this could possibly be so.

"God's Holy Spirit will come to you this night," the angel said. "And God's own Son will be planted within you." And then he told me about my relative Elizabeth and how she too was going to have a baby. This was incredible news to me, since Elizabeth was already quite old and previously unable to have children.

"Nothing is impossible with God!" the angel said.

And so, right there in the garden, I bowed my head and said, "I am pleased to be God's servant! Let it happen as you say." Then the angel vanished quickly as he had come. I stayed there on my knees, eyes closed and head bowed, for a few moments as I pondered over all I had heard. Finally I opened my eyes, and there on the packed ground of the garden path I noticed a small flower seed. Now, most people would overlook such a tiny insignificant thing as a seed. But out of habit I immediately picked it up, tucked it into the little pocket I had sewn into my tunic specifically for that purpose, and then, remembering what had just transpired, I stood and looked around.

At first I thought perhaps I had simply daydreamed this entire happening. But something inside my heart told me it was real. That very night it all occurred just as the angel had promised, and the next morning I knew that miraculously, just as a seed is planted in the mysterious darkness of the fertile earth, I now carried the seed of God's own child within the secret depths of my body.

Imagine my joy and bewilderment as I considered this phenomenon—so unbelievable, so amazing, so totally unheard of. I wondered what I should do next. Who should I tell? Or was I to keep this secret hidden within me for the time being?

But from that moment on, I knew that my life would never be the same. I had no idea how all the things the angel had told me would come to pass, but I knew my journey had begun. And somehow I knew it would be up to God to get me to the final destination.

Of course, I had no idea that the final destination would be this fearful and hopeless place where many of us huddle together in gloom and in doubt. I had no clue that in the end, my son would be publicly scourged like a common criminal, spat upon, and beaten almost beyond recognition. And as if that were not punishment enough—and *punishment for what?* I have asked myself again and again—he was brutally nailed on a cross where he was tortured for hours before he finally gave up his precious and sinless life. And for what? These are the silent questions that beat their fists upon my soul during this darkest of nights. But I must not heed their cries. For my son's sake, I must not give in to despair.

2

It is in the darkest hours of the night when your faith is put to the hardest test. This is as true now as it was thirty-three years ago when I came to the full realization that I was carrying a baby no one in my family or community could possibly understand or even accept. Shortly after my conception, I attempted to explain to my mother the honor of being chosen by God. For some reason, I thought she would be happy for me.

"Mary!" my mother scolded as she slapped a firm lump of dough into a rounded loaf. "You are speaking nonsense, my child. I will hear of no more such talk from you!"

"But it is true," I insisted. "I *am* with child."

I had never seen a look like that in my mother's eyes, but it sliced through me like my father's butchering knife, and it filled my young heart with real fear. "Mary," she said in a quiet but incensed voice, "if you are with child . . . and if it is not the child of your betrothed . . ." She took in a sharp breath that actually seemed to cause her pain. "Then you shame your family and you place yourself in serious peril." Her strong fingers had released their hold on the dough and now gripped me tightly, biting into my arm. "Tell me it is not so!"

I just mutely shook my head. What more could I say? How could I convince her that this was about honor and had nothing to do with shame? Then I remembered another piece of information the angel had given me. "There is something else," I began in a cautious tone. "The angel told me that our cousin Elizabeth is also with child—"

"This is madness, Mary!" She glanced over her shoulder to be sure no one was lurking in our open doorway eavesdropping on our conversation. "Your cousin Elizabeth is well past her childbearing years. And her husband Zacharias is . . ." She lowered her voice and looked uneasy. "He is *unable.*"

"But the angel said—"

"Enough, Mary!" She turned her attention back to her loaves. "Do not speak of this again."

And so I went to bed with a heavy heart that night. For the first time in my life, I believed that my name, Mary, which literally means "bitter," befitted my life. I cried quietly into my shawl as I considered my plight. How was I to bear God's child if even my own mother did not believe me? I was no fool; I understood our laws. An unmarried woman could not be with child and survive. Such women were called horrible names, they were publicly humiliated, and then they were stoned.

Unable to sleep, I quietly rose from my bed, slipped outside, and went to the garden. By the light of the nearly full moon, I found my favorite thinking rock, and there I sat, pondering over my predicament. It was while on that rock that I remembered how Hannah, the faithful mother of the great prophet Samuel, had once poured her heart out to Jehovah, and so I did the same. First I gave thanks for the honor he had bestowed upon me, but then I begged him to deliver me, to protect me. I asked him to show me a way through my wilderness. And just before dawn the answer became as clear as the noontime sun.

I finished my morning chores and waited until my younger sister Sarah had gone to the village well for water and, as always, the latest gossip. Then I made certain my older brothers were busy at work with my father. My plan was to be sure no one was present when I approached my mother. Since my startling announcement the previous day, she had turned distant and moody to all of us, and I knew she was avoiding me in particular. But the house was quiet and still now, and I was more determined than ever to get her full attention.

"Mother," I said in my firmest voice, ready to make the long speech I had already prepared in my mind, "I think you should allow me to travel to see our cousin Elizabeth so that I may—"

"Yes!" she said suddenly, before I had barely begun. She looked up from where she was churning butter. "That is exactly what you will do." She nodded as if it were her own idea. "Prepare yourself to travel to Judah. Your brother Asher will accompany you. You will leave the day after the Sabbath."

I was not sure if she was simply eager to be rid of me, trying to put off the inevitable humiliation she was certain I would bring upon my family, or if she perhaps thought our wise cousin might somehow be able to straighten me out. It was even possible that she wanted me to stay with my cousin indefinitely. I guess I will never know her motives for sure. But I do know that my mother loved me. I could see it plainly in her concerned eyes as she hugged me and bade me shalom just as the sun came up on the morning after Sabbath.

Asher and I walked quietly through the sleepy village of Nazareth, setting our pace for what would be a nearly weeklong journey into the hill country of Judah. I am sure my mother assumed my heart would be somber, heavy with the burden I carried, as we traveled along. But as soon as we reached the outskirts of our hometown, I became light and joyful. To me, the world was a beautiful place filled with the fresh, green scent of springtime and the abundance of wildflowers blooming along the verdant hillsides. To me, life was young and new and promising—God's Son was alive inside me. It was a day to rejoice and be glad!

So different from now—this night that seems to stretch into eternity. I think about him as I sit here in the darkness. I wonder if the lamps we left in the tomb are still burning. I think of his battered body, quickly cleaned as best we could before Sabbath came, then hastily wrapped in fine linen cloth before the Roman soldiers shooed us away and replaced the heavy stone door that blocked the entrance, sealing him off from us. I think of him lying there, alone and beaten, and I wonder, despite my promise to remain faithful, What has Jehovah done?

I remind myself that I must not dwell there. I must not give in to the darkness. And so I continue on my journey. I remember the feeling I had when after days of traveling we finally reached the home of our relatives Elizabeth and Zacharias.

"Asher," I said to my brother, "is this really where they live? It looks like a palace!"

He squinted up against the bright afternoon sun, then nodded. "It is just as Father said in his directions. Surely, you have heard Father say how our relatives are very wealthy. Zacharias is an important priest." Then he handed me my bundle of clothing and smiled. "You will be in good hands here, little one."

"You are not staying?" I asked in alarm.

He grinned and looked down at his grubby clothes. "I am not fine enough to visit such a place."

"But, Asher!" I had no doubts that I appeared just as impoverished as my brother.

"Father told me to hurry back," he said as he turned and waved.

So now I was alone and more than just a little intimidated by the grandeur standing before me. I had not imagined that my relatives were so well off. I did not know anyone this well off. I started to head for the impressive entrance. Then, wanting my first appearance to be acceptable, I turned and went down to a well we had passed on our way through the town. I shook the traveling dust from my outer garments before I washed my hands and face. Then I wet and smoothed my hair and adjusted my veil. I know it was not much, but it was the best I could do.

My father had sent a message ahead, and I knew my relatives would be expecting me. But I had no idea what my reception would be among such grand and educated people. A well-dressed servant met me at the door. I told him my name, and after studying me carefully he finally stepped back and allowed me into the spacious home. I am sure he thought I was a peasant who had no business intruding on Elizabeth and Zacharias's lives like this. Clutching my shabby bundle of clothes to my chest, I waited as he went off in search of his mistress. I noticed then that the floors were made of fitted stone. Perhaps even marble, but I was not sure. The floor in my parents' home was made of hard-packed dirt that was dark and brown, but these floors shone like sunshine in the afternoon light.

"Dear Mary!" A woman who was much older than my mother entered the room. She was dressed like a queen, with her beautiful silver braids coiled around her head like a crown. I actually wondered if I should bow to her. But then I saw her smile, and it felt familiar and genuine.

"Cousin Elizabeth?"

She continued to approach me, then stopped suddenly. Her faded eyes grew wide, and her smile vanished as her brows shot up. "Oh!" she said as she stood there for a moment, clutching her midsection with both hands.

"Are you all right?" I asked as I ran to her. I hoped my arrival was not too unexpected or unsettling for her. "Shall I call for help?"

Then she seemed to relax as she smiled and said, "Dear Mary, you are so blessed among women!" Gently taking my hands in hers, she continued to speak, looking directly into my eyes as if she could see straight into my soul. "And even more blessed is the babe who sleeps in your womb! But why am I so fortunate that the mother of my Lord comes to visit my humble home?"

I was speechless! But at the same time my heart bubbled with joy at her words. Cousin Elizabeth knew what was happening in me! She understood the miracle Jehovah had begun!

"The babe inside me leaped!" she said with moist eyes. "The moment I saw you . . ." Then she took my hand and firmly placed it on her rounded belly. "My son leaped for joy! You have been greatly blessed, dear Mary. You have believed what God has told you. And now every word will come true!"

And it was as if Jehovah himself had removed the cork that had been keeping my words within me, and like a psalm, or perhaps a fountain of praise, they came pouring out of me. Elizabeth laughed and clapped her hands when I finished.

Even now I still remember those words. I know them by heart. Sometimes I repeat them to myself. I think they might help me on this dark and hopeless night. And now, perhaps more than ever before, I am encouraged by the powerful truth. I remind myself that this thing—this thing that mighty Jehovah has begun—is not over yet.

Lord God Jehovah has filled my soul
    to bursting!
And my spirit rejoices in my Savior!
Although I was lowly, he honored
    me—he chose me for his
    handmaid.
And forevermore I shall be called
    blessed!
Jehovah has done great things for
    me, and his name is Holy!
His mercy is poured out on all who
    trust him.
He shows his power and strength
    and tumbles the proud.

He dethrones the mighty and exalts the humble.
He feeds the hungry, but those who think they are rich leave with nothing.
He remembers his chosen Israel, pouring out his mercy!
Just as he has promised—beginning with Abraham and for all eternity!

3

During my visit with Elizabeth, I was treated like a princess. My cousin was so delighted to have my company during the latter part of her pregnancy. Especially since her husband, Zacharias, was unable to speak. I found this strangely intriguing. How could it be that a priest was unable to speak? Then Elizabeth explained how Zacharias had doubted the angel of the Lord when he told him that God planned to bless them with a child.

"My poor husband could not believe that anyone as ancient as he and I could bear children," Elizabeth said, sadly shaking her head. "He doubted God."

I nodded with understanding. After all, that was exactly what my own mother had done.

"And in that moment God struck him mute," Elizabeth said with an amused smile. "As a result, it has been very quiet around here—that is, until you arrived."

Elizabeth made sure I ate healthful foods and got plenty of sleep while in her home. She also shared with me all the knowledge she had been gathering about pregnancy and childbirth. She was the kind of woman who had an unquenchable thirst for knowledge and a love for God that was unsurpassed. To this day, I think of her as one of my finest examples of womanhood, and I am eternally grateful for the influence she had on my life.

She also took me under her wing in regard to my wardrobe. Without insulting my poor peasant girl attire, she helped me make some lovely garments that I later used for my wedding and married life, as well as some fine pieces for my still unborn son. She had an eye for beauty and quality unlike any I had ever seen before.

Being with Elizabeth for all those weeks

was like a priceless gift from God. Her faith and strength and wisdom encouraged me every single day of my visit. And she helped confirm that Jehovah had indeed blessed me with the greatest honor given to women.

"The child in your womb will change the course of history," she told me. And whenever I felt overwhelmed by such strong prophetic words, worried that I, an inexperienced young girl, would be incapable of mothering such an important child, she gently reminded me that the Lord God would show me how to do these things.

"Lean on him, Mary," she often said. "The Lord Jehovah will lead you."

Her genuine love and kind words were like a fortification that strengthened my heart, and after three months passed I felt ready for what lay ahead. I knew it was time to go home.

Elizabeth and I embraced for a long moment when I was about to leave. She was nearly ready to deliver, and her belly was so swollen that I could barely wrap my arms around her. Both of us were crying, tears of joy mixed with tears of sorrow.

"The Lord God Jehovah bless you at your birthing time," I told her as I wiped my eyes. "Blessings upon you and your son and his father."

"And on you," she said, waving a silk scarf as I left her home. "And upon my Lord, your son."

Asher was waiting for me down by the road. Once again he had been too embarrassed to come inside Elizabeth and Zacharias's fine house, although I knew he had gladly taken the food the servant had given him. He appeared to have finished his meal, as he rested in the shade of an olive tree. But when he saw me he stood and waved.

"I think I must be traveling with royalty," he said as he pretended to bow. "Where did you get the new clothes?"

Embarrassed by my finery, I quickly explained that our cousin Elizabeth was very generous.

"I noticed," he said as he nodded to the large bundle the servant had given him to carry for me. I had a smaller bundle of my own.

"Do you mind?" I asked, feeling guilty for being such a burden.

"Not for you, little sister." Then he hugged me and told me he had missed me at home. "And I am not the only one," he said as we began walking north. "Your betrothed is beside himself."

"Joseph?"

He nodded. "Who else? The poor man has asked me at least a dozen times when you planned to come home. I think he was worried that you had left us for good."

Joseph. I had barely considered him during my time away. Not that I did not care about him. I certainly did. But I had no idea how he would react to my rather shocking announcement. Instead of fretting, I reminded myself of Elizabeth's words. *"Trust Jehovah. He will see you through."*

As we walked, I prayed that Jehovah would also see Joseph through. For I knew as well as anyone that Joseph, the strong and handsome carpenter, was indeed a proud man. A good man, no doubt, but any man (no matter how good) would have to question how his betrothed had come to be in the family way and yet remained a virgin. It was clear that I had some explaining to do. *Trust Jehovah, I told myself. He will see me through.*

I remind myself of these same words again tonight. I know that, more than ever, I need to believe this. Trust Jehovah, and he will see me through. Trust Jehovah.

Weary from travel after I got home, I spent a couple of days in solitude and rest—and prayer. But I knew I could not avoid Joseph forever, and on the third day I sent a message through Asher that I wanted to speak to my betrothed. I invited Joseph to meet me in our family's garden, hoping that would keep our conversation private. I even wore one of the new outer garments Elizabeth had helped me create, along with a very fine linen veil and several bracelets. I could tell by Joseph's expression that he was truly happy to see me, and I suspect that my improved appearance was pleasing to him. This did not make the task before me any easier.

After a formal greeting, I decided to speak frankly. I had no flowery speech prepared, no persuasive words to convince him of my innocence. All I knew to do was to simply tell him the truth. And so I did.

Joseph's dark brows drew together, and his face twisted in pain, and perhaps anger, at my words. I knew he did not believe me. Still, he said nothing. He just stared at me in the most accusing way. It reminded me of the look I had received from my mother—only magnified.

"I am sorry that you do not believe me," I began.

"How can I believe you?" he said in a tightly controlled voice, as if each word caused him agony.

I nodded. "Yes, I knew this would be difficult. But I am praying that Jehovah will show you the truth."

"The truth?" He exhaled loudly and folded his arms across his chest as he looked down on me. I could tell by his gaze that he considered me as something dirty, something beneath him, something he would not willingly associate himself with any longer than necessary. "I can see the truth, Mary," he said in a surprisingly calm but sad voice. "You have been away for three long months. You come back wearing fine clothing and gold bracelets, and now you tell me you are with child. The truth is quite obvious."

"That is not—"

He held up his hand to stop my words. "Silent, woman!"

I just nodded and waited for his wrath to continue.

He stood there for a long time, and I could tell that he was thinking, perhaps deciding how he would deal with me. I am sure he assumed that my fate was in his hands. According to our culture, it was. However, I knew that only Jehovah controlled my future. And so I waited.

"I think it is best to handle this as quietly as possible," he finally told me. "You will go away . . . perhaps back to your relatives in the hills of Judah or wherever you have been. We will make an excuse, explaining that there has been a misunderstanding, that I have changed my mind in regard to taking you as—" He actually choked. "As my bride."

Then he turned and walked away.

I tried to remember Elizabeth's words

just then, her admonition to trust Jehovah despite how things might look. But it was not easy.

Perhaps faith is like that—it is *not* easy. But, in a way, it is very simple. We cannot do it by ourselves, that is obvious. But when we turn to the Lord God Jehovah, he gives us what we are lacking—faith. That is where I am tonight. It is *not* easy. Nothing about this excruciating day has been easy. But I will not make it through this night without faith. *Please, Lord, increase my faith that I might survive until morning.*

4

Some nights make you long for the dawn. And yet when the sun finally starts to rise, you want it to be gentle and kind, perhaps veiled by the clouds, easing you into the day that may devour you before it is even half over.

That is how I felt the morning after my conversation with Joseph. I knew he had been gracious, all things considered, but I also knew that this was just the sort of situation where a man might change his mind. For instance, he still had his family to discuss the dissolution of our engagement with. What if they became enraged by what they would surely suspect as my unfaithfulness to him? What if they refused to accept his "excuses" for ending our agreement? There was potential for all sorts of things to go wrong. Still, I tried to remain faithful to Jehovah's plan, making an effort not to dwell on the potential pitfalls. I knew the only thing I could really do was wait.

My mother avoided my eyes that morning. I suspect that she also knew that my future was hanging in the balance, and I suppose she thought she could postpone the inevitable by ignoring me altogether. In fact, it seemed that everyone in my family had been treating me differently since my visit with Elizabeth. Except for Asher, although even he seemed somewhat uncomfortable since we had gotten home.

Fortunately for me, the garden had been neglected during my absence and there was much to be done in order to bring it back into the pristine condition I always tried to maintain. It provided a good distraction for me during that long day of waiting. And as I weeded I tried to stifle any visions of my being dragged through the streets of Nazareth by Joseph's indignant family and then thrown down before the village priests and elders as I was accused of my crime—fornication or possibly adultery, since our engagement was a legally binding commitment—and then given my sentence. But sometimes, when I least expected it, this image would flash through my mind with the speed of a cast stone, and all I could do was take in a deep breath and pray.

I am sure I jumped when I heard Joseph saying my name.

"Mary?"

I dropped the piece of twine that I had been about to use to tie up the grape vine that was hanging down in the dirt. Still stooped down like an animal caught in a trap, I glanced over my shoulder. Part of me expected to see his angry brothers clustered behind him, ready to dish out my fate. But Joseph appeared to be alone.

"Joseph," I said calmly as I stood straight, wiping my dusty hands on the sides of one of my older tunics, not nearly so fine as what I had worn the night before. Then I pushed a fallen strand of hair back beneath my veil and held my shoulders back and waited.

"Mary," he said again, but the tone of his voice was gentle. And then, to my utter astonishment, he fell down on both knees before me, taking my right hand in his. "I am so sorry."

"For what?" I asked, longing for him to get back to his feet.

"For not believing you."

I felt my eyes growing large. "But you do believe me now?"

He nodded. "An angel of the Lord appeared to me last night. It was incredible, Mary. He told me that all that you said is true. He told me many things. He even told me what we are to name our son."

"*Our* son?" I felt tears filling my eyes. I went down on my knees in front of Joseph.

"Yes, Mary, *our* son. We will soon be married, and you will give birth to the Son of God, just as you told me, and I will take care of both of you."

"Oh, Joseph!"

Now, in all honesty, I can say that this is the very moment when I really began to love this man. And this was a love that grew and grew over the years. I know now it was no mistake that God chose sweet Joseph to be my husband and to help me raise and care for our son.

"I am so sorry," he said again, and I saw that tears were filling his eyes. "I will never doubt you again."

We both slowly rose to our feet, and then we embraced. I still remember the feeling of his strong arms around me. I knew that this good man was able to protect me. I remember the deep sigh of relief that escaped my lips just then.

And then we stepped apart. I think we were both slightly embarrassed by our first open display of affection for one another. But I knew that something miraculous had happened in that moment. I knew that God had knit our hearts together as one. And just as I felt encouraged when my cousin Elizabeth had believed in me, I felt even more so now with my betrothed.

"We will marry as soon as possible," Joseph told me as I wiped my tears.

"Joseph?" I said suddenly.

"Yes, dear one?"

"What is his name?"

"Jesus," Joseph said with authority. "His name is to be called Jesus." Then he looked down upon me with the most tender expression I had ever seen, and I knew without doubt that my future would be safe in the hands of this man—and in the hands of Jehovah.

Tonight, as much as I longed for that unwavering strength of my good and gentle husband, I am thankful that Joseph did not have to witness the events of this awful day. I fear it would have broken his heart completely. For Joseph always loved Jesus just as dearly as if he had been his own flesh and blood. In fact, there were times when our other children accused their father of favoritism. But then I suppose all children fret about this sort of nonsense.

But I know that if Joseph had been alive to see what happened in Jerusalem today, he would have thrown himself at the Roman guards who were mercilessly beating Jesus. He would have attempted to stop them, and I am sure he would have even tried to take Jesus's torture upon himself. That is how much he loved our son. And it would have killed him. I wonder if my Joseph watched these atrocities from paradise today. And, if he could see, I wonder if he, like me, still weeps.

5

They say that tears last for the night but joy comes in the morning. I fear that is not true today. For even as the sky changes from slate to pale gray, I feel no joy. Only a vast, sad emptiness that fills every corner of my soul. No one is stirring as I slip out to the terrace to view the breaking of the dawn. I am slightly surprised that the sun has even risen today. I am disturbed that it has the nerve to show its face around here after the Son of God was put to death only yesterday. There is some satisfaction in seeing a thick layer of clouds obscuring much of the light. Perhaps those clouds might even bring rain. I do not think I can abide a cheerful blue sky today.

I sit down on a bench and force my mind to remember another day that I can dwell in for a while. I recall another time when I rose early like this to greet the dawn. Indeed, that was a happy day. It brimmed with hope and expectation, and I could not wait for it to begin. Now, you might think my wedding day was a somber and anticlimactic affair, especially after all that Joseph and I had been through. But that is not how I saw it. Not at all! I welcomed that day with an open heart—I could not wait for the festivities to begin.

I am certain my parents were greatly relieved that Joseph and I were going ahead with our wedding. And when Joseph asked to push the day forward, he received no resistance from my parents. In some ways it was as if the entire town was relieved. My sister Sarah said there had been rumors circulating at the well, but, being a loyal sister, she did all she could to stifle them. And, apparently, her efforts paid off, for everyone seemed thoroughly glad that Joseph and I were celebrating our nuptials.

It was not a large wedding, but it was a joyous one. I wore my finest clothes and even the gold bracelets and earrings Elizabeth had given me for this special day. We had plenty of good food and music and wine, and our guests remained happy and stayed long into the night. Indeed, our wedding was remembered as one of Nazareth's happiest affairs. It was even on this occasion when Sarah's future husband first noticed her. He was a merchant from Cana, and Sarah still claims it was because he was so impressed with my wedding that he pursued her. But at the time I reminded her that she was becoming a beautiful young woman.

She laughed. "If only I could grow to be half as beautiful as you."

"Silly girl," I told her. "You are already twice as lovely."

But I suppose I actually did feel beautiful on my wedding day. I had no illusions about my physical appearance, for I have never considered myself a beauty. But I did feel truly beautiful on the inside. I am sure that, more than anything else, this had to do with the secret blessing that slept within my womb. But I was surprised when numerous friends and relatives proclaimed my beauty with happy toasts. Of course, some of them were feeling the afterglow of the music and wine, but I received their compliments with grace, smiling quietly to myself.

Yet it was the expression on Joseph's face that I will always remember about that day. It was a certain moment as we stood beneath the canopy and said our vows. It was an unforgettable look of true love and adoration. I have no doubt that I was truly beautiful in my husband's eyes that day and always. However, I must admit to feeling a bit guilty, or maybe it was just sympathy for my dear bridegroom, when he finally took me to the sweet little house he had prepared for us right next to his widowed mother's home.

He had somehow found the time to create several well-made pieces of furniture for our own use—a low table, a bench and a stool, and a lovely carved trunk. The small space was clean and orderly. But when I saw the bed off in the corner, a sturdy pallet constructed, I knew, by my beloved's own two hands, I looked at him with troubled eyes. To my relief, he simply laughed.

"No need to worry, dear Mary," he said in a reassuring voice. "The angel made it very clear that I am not to take you as my wife until after God's Son is born. And, have no fear, I am prepared to wait for you."

I reached out and hugged him, telling him once again how much I loved him.

"But know this," he said as he took my face into his two hands. "I greatly look forward to that day, my love."

So it was that we slept together side by side in our wedding bed without having sexual relations. And so it continued for the next six months. I knew that Joseph loved me and even that he desired me in the way a husband desires his wife. But not one time did he pressure me. Not only was Joseph a good man, but he had more integrity than any man I have ever known—even my own father, and I always felt that no one would ever measure up to him.

But here is what I still find very interesting as I recall those first months of our marriage—during that time of restraint and self-control, my husband and I became very intimate. Not on a physical level, of course. Although, it was amusing how everyone in our families assumed we were physically intimate and even teased us for looking so happy all the time. But we drew very close on a deep emotional level—or perhaps it was spiritual. All I knew was that it was a level of intimacy I had never experienced before. Nor do I expect to experience it again.

My sweet Joseph. Jehovah knew exactly what he was doing when he chose this dear man to be my husband and Jesus's earthly father. The Lord God made no mistake in selecting Joseph the carpenter of Nazareth. Sometimes I even wonder if God did not choose Joseph first and then me later. I remember telling Joseph this very thing once, and he laughed so hard. Of course, he told me I had it all backward.

Even so, I have marveled at how some (those who believe in my son's deity) have treated me with such awe-filled reverence and respect—and really it was Joseph who wielded the most earthly influence on Jesus's life. In some ways, I was only the earthen vessel that poured God's Son into his human life. But it was Joseph who cared for us and provided for us, who protected us, and who faithfully taught Jesus everything from the Shema to how to make a perfectly fitting oxen yoke. Perhaps someday people will acknowledge my Joseph, honoring him for all he so willingly contributed to God's own Son. Or maybe not. Maybe we shall all be forgotten, blown away like the chaff from the grain. It is so hard—even in the light of day—not to give in, not to surrender to this cloak of despair.

Others are awake now. And soon we gather together in the gloomy rooms of this gloomy home that is feeling more and more like a prison to me, but little is said. What is left to say? Finally some of us decide we must return to the tomb and see for ourselves what has happened. We are like lost children as several of us silently slip outside and toward my son's final resting place. We know it is Sabbath and most would consider it a sin for us to make this short journey. But we cannot help ourselves. We need to know.

Once we are far enough away not to be observed, we speak in hushed tones, trying to encourage each other, reminding one another of things Jesus once said, promises he made. But our words emerge flat and without hope, lifelessly hanging in the chilly morning air.

Finally we reach the tomb, but all is the same as yesterday. The centurion guards are still at their post, although we suspect we have startled them, for they suddenly jump to attention. But when they realize it is only us, they make a couple of jeers, and then, because we offer them no encouragement, they turn to each other and make jokes at our expense.

It is clear that the stone is unmoved. It remains securely positioned over the opening just as it was yesterday. Even the seal is untouched, unbroken. Nothing has changed. We turn away feeling even more lost than before. No one speaks as we return to where we are staying—what seems to be turning into our own sort of tomb.

How long must we wait, Jehovah? How long? And why have you done this to us? To your own beloved Son? Why? These are my private thoughts. I do not reveal my personal fears or doubts to the others. For the sake of my son, I shall remain strong—if only on the outside.

Later on, John, a beloved disciple, reminds the others of what my son recently said—*"I shall be gone from you for a while, but let not your heart be troubled, do not be afraid."* I take great comfort in these words. I know that my son always told the truth. Indeed, he proclaimed himself to be the Truth. And, really, I have no reason to doubt him. In all honesty, it is Jehovah who has me worried right now. I still cannot imagine how he allowed all this to happen.

6

Was it only a week ago that I told my dear friend the other Mary that I still feel like a fifteen-year-old girl on the inside? And how true it was then. But now I feel as if I am one hundred years old—no, much, much older. I feel like I have been trudging on this ancient earth since the beginning of time. My soul is weary as a stone, and my feet are aching and tired. I fear that I am too old to continue like this much longer.

I do remember another time when I felt almost this fatigued—although it was purely a physical kind of weariness. At the time I was young and healthy and my spirit was strong with high expectations. I knew it was close to my birthing time when Caesar Augustus made his proclamation that all citizens must be registered at the birthplace of the patriarch of each family. Joseph had been born in Bethlehem, the City of David, and so it was decided that we would travel there together. I did not mind the prospect of this journey. I had always wanted to see Bethlehem, just south of Jerusalem, and besides, almost everyone was on the road going somewhere. It was nearly as festive as Passover.

Joseph, extremely concerned for my welfare, purchased a donkey, which we could barely afford, so I could ride during portions of our journey. He thought he had given us plenty of time to travel, and we stopped frequently so I could rest, but when we finally reached Bethlehem late in the evening, we discovered there were no vacant rooms to be had. I knew I was experiencing birthing pains—indeed, I had been feeling them off and on since midafternoon, although I had kept this to myself since Joseph was already quite worried. But as we entered Bethlehem, I knew that my baby, God's Son, would wait no longer. The child was demanding to be born.

"It is time," I told Joseph in an urgent voice as he returned from inquiring about a room. "The baby is coming."

He nodded. "I know. And I have found us a place to stay." He made a half smile. "I wish it was something better, Mary, but it is the best I can do."

"Anything will be better than having God's Son born out here on the road," I told him. And so it was we found ourselves sharing space with donkeys and oxen and even a few nesting chickens. But, looking back, I think the humble stable was preferable to being in a crowded inn where we surely would have been forced to share space with strangers. And, although the acrid scent of animals was strong in the air, it was not as objectionable to me as the stench of sweaty travelers packed into a stuffy room. In fact, the smell of manure and hay almost reminded me of the earthy smell of my garden. Or so I told myself.

"This is perfect," I assured my worried husband.

He lit an oil lamp and found fresh straw to make a bed in the most protected corner of the stable. He covered the straw with the woolen blankets we had carried with us. I did my best to make myself comfortable and even attempted to sleep between the birthing pains, but soon it was time to push the baby from my womb.

I prayed for mercy as I squatted and attempted to relax my muscles, just as my mother had instructed me to do in the quick birthing lesson she gave me shortly before we left Nazareth. And then, when the moment seemed right, I bore down hard, gripping my husband's hand until I actually saw him wince. He later told me he only winced because he knew I was in such pain.

Then, after several unsuccessful pushes and feeling that this child might never be born, I cried out to Jehovah for strength, and it was in the very next push that I felt something give within me, and I knew the child was emerging. Joseph seemed to know exactly what to do as he caught and then cradled the slippery babe in his strong hands. He had even brought along a clean knife to sever the cord. He confessed afterward that my mother had spoken to him as well. Wise woman, my mother.

Confident that both my son and I were in good hands, I fell quickly to sleep and was surprised to later awaken to the sound of infant cries. But then I remembered. My son was rubbed clean and wrapped with the soft linen cloths I had packed specifically for that use. Joseph had even created a makeshift cradle from one of the feeding mangers. He padded the rough wooden trough first with straw and then soft hay, then lined it with a blanket folded several times over. A perfect little bed!

He smiled proudly as he placed the squirming bundle of life into my arms. And then, holding up his hands and looking to the heavens, Joseph proclaimed our son's name aloud. "We will call him Jesus." Then my husband knelt in an act of worship and said, "Glory be to the Son of the

Most High. He will deliver his people from evil."

As if in a dream, I studied the small, wrinkled red face and the downy-soft swirls of hair. I counted the delicate fingers, examining each perfectly formed nail. And I cannot deny that those wide, dark eyes looking up at me with such trust were truly amazing. But then it always seems nothing short of miraculous when a total and complete human being emerges so perfect from the womb. Even so, when I gazed down at this tiny bundle resting in my arms, all I saw was a baby. A beautiful baby, no doubt. What mother does not think so? But he did not look particularly holy. There was no angelic aura about him, and he smelled perfectly human to this mother's nose. And so I took him to my breast and thanked God for granting me such a divine gift.

This is not to make this event seem ordinary. Believe me, nothing was ordinary about the night my son was born. First of all, both Joseph and I had noticed the most incredible star lighting up the cobalt sky. We were amazed at its shimmering brilliance, unlike anything we had seen before or since, and we felt certain that it was a sign from Jehovah—as if to announce that his Son was coming into the world.

And then, of course, there were the shepherds. They arrived quite suddenly in the middle of the night. Wide-eyed and with grass in their hair, they fell to their knees to worship our son. At first I was astonished that they had even known what was happening or how to find us, but then they explained how angels—many, many angels—had appeared to them on the hillside, waking them from a sound sleep to announce that a king and savior had been born and to tell them where to find us.

Joseph laughed after the shepherds finally departed, saying, "Blessed be our Lord, Mary. Look at how our mighty God resists the proud and reveals himself to the humble."

I smiled at our temporary abode in the lowly stable. "That certainly describes us, does it not?"

"Yes, my love. Jehovah is a good and gracious God."

I marveled at so many things that night. And while my son seemed a normal infant to me—he did not speak or sing or glow with heavenly light—I had no doubt that he was indeed the Son of God. And, yes, it is true, I worshiped him too.

I still do. Even as his body lies lifeless in the tomb, he is still my King. And somehow, despite this troubling doubt that I fight so hard to dispel, I know he will be my Savior. Jehovah's ways are not my ways, but I must trust him. In time he will deliver—just as he has always done.

7

It is impossible to pretend that my son's innocent blood was not shed yesterday. And although I must attempt to be strong for the others, I cannot forget how I stood in the crowd and watched as the Roman soldiers whipped and scourged my son. I cannot erase the dark red streak that flowed from his body and stained the ground below. What mother could bear to see her child bleeding? What mother would not run with a clean cloth in hand and press it to the wound, saying, "There, there, it will be all right"?

But I was not allowed this most basic of mothers' privileges yesterday. I was held at a distance, merely another face in the crowd, cringing inwardly with each wicked blow.

I remember the first time my son's blood was shed. On the eighth day after Jesus's birth, Joseph announced it was time for his circumcision. Now, I had never questioned the customs of my people when it came to this practice. Why would I? It was only with my own lovely child about to go under the priest's knife that I seriously doubted the wisdom of this law. Of course, Joseph assured me that Jesus would be perfectly fine and that this operation had been done thousands of times on thousands of male babies and none had died from it yet. At least none that he knew of.

Still, I fretted a bit as I waited for Joseph to return with my son. And, in all fairness, it was the first time I had been separated from my infant child. But then, while sitting there, something occurred to me with such power and peace that I believed it came from Jehovah himself, and I knew in my heart that this baby was not only my son but also God's beloved Son, and, of course, the Lord God was watching and protecting his own. With a calm spirit, I smiled as Joseph emerged with my child in his arms.

We had to remain in Bethlehem up until the time for my purification. But those were restful and quiet weeks, and Joseph saw to it that my son and I were perfectly comfortable, getting us a room at the inn as soon as the census was completed and travelers returned to their homes.

Even so, I was greatly relieved when my forty days of confinement were completed and it was time to go to Jerusalem. Our money had dwindled during this time away from home, and when we reached the temple and I needed to purchase my purification sacrifice, we could only afford a pair of turtledoves.

I saw the sorrowful look on my husband's face, but I smiled, hoping to reassure him. "Have no doubt, my dear," I said. "The Lord God Jehovah will honor my offering today."

Joseph laughed. "Yes, I think you are right."

When Joseph paid his fee to redeem

our son, we smiled at each other over the irony of this ritual. Then Joseph whispered in my ear, "We are paying to redeem the Redeemer."

Just as we were ready to leave, an astonishing thing happened. A godly old man named Simeon approached us with the light of God dancing in his eyes. He spoke to us as a true prophet, and tears of joy ran down my cheeks as this old man rejoiced that he was finally able to see the real Messiah, proclaiming for all who were listening of how this child, this chosen one, would bring God's salvation and glory to Jerusalem.

Suddenly the old man grew more serious, and, peering directly into my eyes, he spoke of misunderstanding and rejection, and finally he told me that a sword would be thrust through my heart. At those words, I felt a chill run through my soul. Not that I was so concerned for my own welfare, but what about that of my dear son? I clutched my baby closer to my breast as I took in a sharp breath.

Then, to my relief, an ancient-looking woman named Anna came over to us. We heard someone say she was a respected prophetess. With great intensity she studied our child for a long moment, as if seeing something we had missed. And suddenly she lifted her hands and broke out into a beautiful song of worship and praise. She thanked God for sending the one who would free Jerusalem. And with her words came a feeling of peace and joy.

I never forgot Simeon's warning. In fact, those words have echoed through my soul again and again these past two days. And the old prophet was right. A sword has been thrust into my heart. And there it remains. I remember my son's words yesterday as he was hanging on the cross. *"My God, my God, why have you abandoned me?"*

And, while I confess this to no one, this is how I feel today. Abandoned. Even so, I will not give up hope. I will not surrender to despair.

In the same way that my ancestors have encouraged themselves for generations, by retelling the old stories of faith and deliverance, I will continue to remember my own stories. I will continue to relive the many times when Jehovah came through.

We returned to Bethlehem after our trip to Jerusalem. We planned to have a brief rest, collect our things, and then to travel home to Nazareth. How I longed to return to my hometown! Certainly, some say that Nazareth is not much of a town. Or that Galilee is not much of a region. But it was everything to me. Besides that, my family had not yet seen our new son. I could not wait to travel.

But Jehovah had other plans for us. Of course, this thought forces me back into the present. For it seems that Jehovah always has other plans. What is new about that?

I go and sit by the window, watching as the younger women, the two other Marys and several others, keep themselves busy with food preparations and menial household tasks. These chores would normally not be done on the Sabbath, but everyone was too consumed with the grief of the crucifixion yesterday, and things went undone. Besides, we have sat under Jesus's teachings long enough to understand that

Sabbath law was meant not to shackle us but to free us. And whether we are hungry or not, our bodies need some nourishment today.

The women say very little to one another as they peel cucumbers and slice bread, but there is a quiet congeniality among them as they work. Once again I feel the outsider, and I even question why I have remained here among them. My own family is still in Jerusalem. I could be staying with them. But, after yesterday, all I knew was to return to this place with the women.

Still, how I long to join the women as they work, to be able to distract myself with the kind of mundane chores my hands can easily perform, and possibly to forget—at least for a moment—why we are all here, gathered together and waiting so endlessly. But John, who seems to be in charge, at least for now, has made it clear that I am to rest. I know this is his way to honor me, and I know he understands that my spirit is downcast, but how much better it would be to keep my hands busy when my heart is aching so.

Still, I must respect John's role. For it was only yesterday, as we stood at the foot of the cross, when my son looked down upon me and, despite his anguish and pain, spoke to us with clarity.

"Woman," he said to me, "this is your son." Then, gasping for breath and moving his pain-stricken gaze to his favorite disciple, he said, "John, this is your mother."

I knew in that moment that his end was coming soon. I also knew this was his way of ensuring that his earthly mother would be cared for after he was gone. But I was struck by something else, something I am still not ready to face. Something that slices through me as painfully as the sword old Simeon spoke of more than thirty-three years ago. But not now, I cannot face this now.

And so I turn my attention away from where the women are working, and I return to another time when Jehovah disappointed me. Perhaps it is not fair to think of it like that. Suffice it to say that once again I did not get my way. But then, as I have mentioned, Jehovah's ways are higher than mine, and, as always, his ways are right and sure and true. It is a pity I cannot always remember that.

So just as I was beginning to feel homesick for Nazareth and growing excited at the prospects of leaving Bethlehem to journey north, we had a most interesting group of visitors. While we were still at the inn, we were told that someone was there to see us. To our surprise, it was three scholarly men who had been traveling for some time in search of the king whose star had shown so brightly on the night of Jesus's birth.

Of course, we gladly showed them our son, and these impressive-looking men, wearing fine garments of richly dyed silk, fell to their knees and worshiped him. Then they gave us valuable gifts of fine gold and rare spices and warned us that Herod was now aware of the birth of a new king.

"Your leader is threatened by your son, and he plans to make a decree that all baby boys in and around Bethlehem be put to death," they informed us. "You must flee the country at once."

That is why our plans to return to Nazareth were postponed. Of course, I could not complain, since our unexpected journey to Egypt was to protect our son. And I must say that I came to enjoy our time there. In many ways, it was as if Joseph and I were newly married, for the time had finally come when we were allowed to live together as husband and wife. And, my, how we both enjoyed our nuptials! Indeed, we were a happy little newlywed family of three.

It was during this relatively peaceful era that I had time to ponder all the miraculous things God had done for us. And I remember one day when the three of us were enjoying a picnic and I asked Joseph what had first made him come to my father asking for my hand in marriage.

"What attracted you to a scrawny young girl like me?" I said as I placed a delicate chain of wildflowers on Jesus's head like a crown.

First Joseph made a joke about how I looked to be a sturdy girl and able to work hard, but then he grew more serious. "Do you remember that old woman who came through town a few years back? I believe some of the townsfolk called her Crazy Azuba."

"Yes!" I said. Of course I remembered this old woman—I had spoken to her and felt sorry for her. "She had no family and stayed down by the well for a few days."

He nodded. "Most of our neighbors shunned her. Probably because of some of the strange things she said."

"I think she was just lonely and desperate."

"I agree. And one day I saw young Mary sneaking food to her. You had it hidden beneath your tunic, and I am sure you thought no one was looking as you slipped it into the old woman's hands."

I felt my cheeks growing warm at this memory. Later that same day I had been made to confess my transgressions to my mother and was then punished for stealing our family's food. Even when I told her I had planned to skip meals for the next two days to make up for the loss, she was still angry at me.

"I got in trouble for it."

He smiled. "So I heard."

"The curse of living in a small town," I said. "Everyone knows everything."

"But your kindness stopped me. It made me pause to really look at you. And when I looked, I liked what I saw."

I felt a lump growing in my throat. To think that my actions—ones that had landed me in such trouble—had actually been what attracted this good man's attention . . . Well, it was just too much to consider.

"Thank you," I told him in a shy voice, suddenly feeling a bit like that insecure thirteen-year-old girl again.

"Thank *you,* Mary." And with Jesus soundly sleeping, we finished off our conversation with a long embrace.

So, you see, I actually became rather fond of our vagabond lifestyle during our exiled period. The sights I was blessed to see during those times! Even now I look back upon it all with fondness. As always, Jehovah knew what was best for us. And during this time I learned to trust him even more. Of course, it helped to have those gifts of gold and spices, worth enough to purchase our housing and food for some time. And Joseph, being a skilled carpenter and very industrious, was always able to find work no matter where we went. I am sure this is just one of the many reasons God chose Joseph to help care for us.

Joseph also proved to be a good balance for me in regard to raising our young son. I suppose I was somewhat overprotective of young Jesus during those early years. I tried to remember that he belonged to God. But sometimes it was not easy. When he started to toddle, I worried each time he took a stumble, afraid he might fall and injure his head. Or if we were near the water, I fretted that he might tumble in and sink like a rock and drown.

"Come on, Mary," Joseph would tease. "Do you really believe the Lord God Almighty would allow harm to come to this little one? Surely if Jesus fell into the river right now, the angels would swoop down from heaven to rescue him, and the child would be perfectly dry before he was safe in your arms again."

"That may very well be," I would answer. "But I believe that the Lord God

Almighty has entrusted his precious Son into my care, and I do not want to appear to be a negligent mother." And so I always kept a diligent eye on my child when he was small. Perhaps it was not so much a matter of fear as it was a matter of responsibility. I may have been young and somewhat inexperienced in the ways of motherhood, but I took my role as Jesus's mother very seriously.

Although I enjoyed our adventures abroad, I was extremely relieved to learn of Herod's death. It meant the end of our forced exile and a joyful return to our hometown in Nazareth. And what a homecoming we had. My younger sister was just preparing for her wedding, and everyone was so happy to see us.

I think our absence helped our situation. It was almost as if my mother had forgotten all about the unbelievable confession I had made to her nearly three years earlier. I am sure she wanted to forget it, since, at the time, she had thought I was crazy.

And yet I still recall moments when I would catch her looking at Jesus, her brows pinched together in consternation as she studied her grandson closely, and I am sure she was wondering . . . although she never said as much and we never discussed it again.

Jesus was weaned about the same time we returned to Nazareth, and it was not long before other children came along. And soon I was greatly occupied with all that came with caring for little ones and running an efficient household. To be perfectly honest, I became so busy with my responsibilities in our home that I sometimes forgot, or quite nearly forgot, that my eldest child was in reality the Son of God. In this mother's eyes, he was a very normal little boy who cried when he skinned his knee and did not enjoy having me wash that stubborn dirt that always wedged itself behind his ears.

However, I do remember a time when he did something that touched this mother's heart in a deep way. But I do not believe it was anything inspired. Or was it? As I recall, Jesus was about four years old at the time. I often took him to the garden with me, for, just like me when I was a child, he delighted in green growing things. But on this particular day we were walking to market, and he stopped abruptly in the middle of the busy street and stooped down to pick something up. I thought it was probably a colorful stone or maybe even a lost coin, but when he stood he had a tiny mustard seed in his hand. But the way he held it up to me was as if he had just found the greatest treasure.

"It will grow into something big, Mother," he proclaimed proudly, almost as if he were already a gardening expert.

Then he very reverently handed me the seed, to be kept safe in my little seed pocket until we got home. Now, I am sure he only did this because he had seen me doing it. But the expression of pure delight on his round face will always be one of my favorite memories of him during child-hood. Later that day we planted the seed in a pot just for him, and he cared for it until it grew into quite a nice large mustard plant that always yielded many mustard seeds.

Of course, it was easy to see that Jesus was an intelligent boy, always mature for his age and very responsible. I could trust him to watch his younger siblings and know that everything would be under control. But in many ways, this was not so unusual for a firstborn child. Sometimes people would comment on what a fine young man Jesus was becoming. "So respectful, so wise for his years," they would say. Some would even say he was "special" in a way that suggested he had a deep spirituality, as if they expected he might go into the priesthood or perhaps become a scribe or fulfill some other high calling that would serve God.

That is when I would remember that my son was indeed very special. More special than our friends and neighbors could possibly imagine. But, for the most part, it was as if this was a secret I kept hidden in my heart—along with so many other things.

During these recent years, when Jesus came into the full realm of his ministry, I have often been asked by believers if his childhood was unusual. "Did he do miracles as a boy?" they will ask. "Did he ever heal a bird or a lamb?" And I must shake my head and admit that his boyhood, in most ways, was perfectly normal.

Well, except for one thing—and not a small thing either. This was a boy who never sinned. To be honest, I was not even fully aware of this until recently. I think I merely considered him to be a very good boy. A noble son that anyone would be proud of, a young man with great integrity, a child you could trust to *always* tell the truth. Now, it was not that I had ever imagined he had sinned, but then he was not exactly what you would think of as angelic either. He never acted superior, and he certainly never lorded over anyone. He could laugh and play just like the other children. But, unlike the other children, he never treated anyone with the slightest trace of malice, and he never showed a speck of envy. How I wish I could say that of my other children!

I suppose it was only natural for Jesus's younger siblings to feel jealous of their eldest brother. Not that he ever gave them reason. If anything, he was exceedingly patient and kind to all of them. And most of the time I believe they truly loved their brother. But it could not have been easy for them to follow after him. It was impossible for them to ever measure up. And, while it is perfectly normal for a father to take his first son into business with him, I could not help but notice the resentment of Jesus's younger brothers when they did not get the same measure of attention Jesus received. I hope they do not forget how they got it later, after my Joseph died and Jesus took over the role of spiritually guiding them and teaching them the ways of carpentry.

Sometimes I even worried that Jesus was spending too much time helping our family. There was no denying that we needed his assistance, but even so, I felt concerned for God's purpose for him here on earth. When was the Messiah to make himself known? When would his kingdom begin? When would he receive the honor due to the Son of God? How it grieves me to think of this now. Had I known that his path was taking him straight to his death,

I never would have wished for it to begin. I would have patiently bided my time, relishing each living moment still spent in his presence.

8

Our lives flowed into a relatively uneventful pattern during our first ten years back in Nazareth. As I mentioned, I was busily seeing to the needs of my family, almost unaware that we had a piece of God living in our midst. Although, I do recall a certain Passover, more than two decades ago now, when I received a vivid reminder of who my firstborn son really was—or rather *whose* he was.

As was our custom, we had traveled down to Jerusalem to celebrate the Passover. Not unlike my children, I welcomed the change of pace this annual pilgrimage offered. Of course, the preparation involved work, but it was happy work, and once we were on our way I was always reminded of my own girlhood days and how excited my sister and I would become at the thrill of a new adventure on the road. As usual, we traveled in the company of family and friends and neighbors, and, as usual, the children usually ran free and sometimes a bit wild.

Yet even when I made this journey as a mother with my large brood of children, I never concerned myself too greatly over their safety or welfare. I knew that between our neighbors and relatives, my children would be well looked after. It was the same way I watched over my sister Sarah's two little girls when they latched onto me, as they so often did, begging me to tell them stories of our adventures in Egypt. To them Aunt Mary was something of an experienced traveler.

And, most assuredly, I *never* worried about Jesus. By this time, he was nearly an adult, not to mention a very responsible and trustworthy young man. Naturally, we had no reason to concern ourselves over his actions. Now, our young Joses, on the other hand, actually fell into mischief a time or two during these trips. Although, it was nothing we could not easily sort out eventually.

As is the usual case, after being away for a couple of weeks, I looked forward to going home again. For although I liked the adventure, I welcomed the thought of being back under my own roof, eating from my own garden, and sleeping in the bed made by my husband's strong hands. And so I was happy when it was finally time to leave Jerusalem.

It was early in the morning when we began our journey back to Nazareth. But by that same afternoon, I realized that I had yet to see my eldest son. "Joseph!" I called toward the front of our traveling group, where most of the men were walking together, discussing important things like politics and the future of our people. "Have you seen Jesus?"

It quickly became obvious that Jesus was nowhere among our group. Joseph immediately offered to return to Jerusalem on his own to search for our missing son. But I knew I would be at my wits' end if I did not go with him. My family offered to keep our other children with them as they continued toward home, hoping to meet up with us later. Meanwhile, Joseph and I hastened back to the city.

We searched where we had been staying but found no sign of him or even anyone who had seen him. We went to the various sites around town, looking around the numerous pools and public gardens as well as the marketplace, but by nightfall we had not found our son.

I know that neither of us slept much that night. And although I prayed to Jehovah, asking him to protect his Son and to keep watch over him, I still fretted over Jesus's safety. It was so unlike him to worry us like this. It seemed the only reason for such distress must be an unfortunate disaster of some kind. Unwelcome images of my beloved son, injured in some way, flashed like uncontrollable lightning bolts through my mind. Perhaps he had been run down by a careless soldier's horse. The Romans have always been so inconsiderate of our people. Or maybe he had eaten something bad and fallen ill and was now lying along the street somewhere, stricken with fever and thirsting for a cup of cool water. Only my prayers could quiet my fearful heart, but even then I was uneasy and without sleep.

It was not until the following day when we went to the temple that we noticed an impressive young man with a group of teachers and elders gathered attentively around him. Then, upon second look, we realized that the young man was our son!

Well, I ran over right to where Jesus was standing, and, interrupting my son in mid-sentence, I demanded to know what he was doing. "Do you not know that your father and I have been sick with worry for you?" I said rather loudly. "We've been all over Jerusalem looking everywhere for you!"

"Why were you looking for me?" he said calmly. "Did you not realize I would be right here taking care of my Father's business?"

While I knew this was not any form of back talk or disrespect, it hurt just the same—almost like a slap in the face. His Father's business? I remember pondering his explanation as we hurried out of town, hoping we might catch up with our traveling companions and abandoned children. What kind of business could that possibly be? After all, Jesus was only twelve—a mere boy, really. Still, I hid his words, like I have hidden so many other things, as if they are seeds planted deeply within my heart. Perhaps one day they will all sprout and grow into something that makes more sense.

But not today, I am thinking as I sit here listening to John reminding us of the words my son said only days ago. "Do you not remember," John says with enthusiasm that is easily betrayed by the sadness in his eyes, "Jesus said that he was going somewhere, somewhere we cannot follow, but that he was sending a helper back to us—a loyal friend who will guide us to the truth."

"Maybe we should go looking for this friend," another disciple suggested.

"No, we need to stay put," someone else said.

And soon they were arguing. Some felt we should search for this helper person immediately. Some felt we should stay hidden here lest someone else in our group be arrested and put to death. Others, mostly the women, wanted to go wait at the tomb.

We are like small children on our way to Passover, except that we have no parent to lead or watch over us. We are lost, truly lost. Or, more appropriately, we are like sheep. I remember how my son used to compare us to sheep—not a very flattering image, since everyone knows that sheep are the most senseless of all domesticated animals. But then Jesus would explain how he was our shepherd. And we never doubted this, for while he was here he was an excellent shepherd. But now he is gone, and we are very, very lost.

After that incident at Passover, I watched Jesus more carefully. But not so you would notice, for I did not want to make him uncomfortable. Not that he was ever uncomfortable, not to my knowledge anyway. But from time to time I would find myself just staring at him, wondering what this was all about and how Jehovah planned to reveal the true identity of this tall and handsome young man. But one year blended into another and nothing spectacular happened.

To be honest, there was one moment when I wished that Jesus was not God's Son. I am not proud of this, but it is true. In fact, I briefly entertained thoughts that perhaps I had imagined the whole thing all those many years ago. But, in all fairness, it was a dark day for me when this happened. And I told no one (except for Jehovah, to whom I had to confess and repent) that I was such a selfish woman.

It was on the day that my dear Joseph died. Suddenly I felt so alone and overwhelmed at the prospects of providing for and raising my half-grown children. How my heart ached from missing my Joseph! But at the same time, Jesus was such a comfort to me. No mother ever had such a loyal and tender son. My other children, equally grief stricken over the loss of their father, were in need of reassurance. And it is a mother's place to offer this condolence to her children.

But when I found myself alone in my garden, quietly grieving as I mourned the loss of my beloved husband, it was Jesus who met me there. And as I looked at my son through eyes blurred with tears, I saw the compassion of the almighty Jehovah on his face. And, like me, Jesus was crying. We embraced, and it was as if I was being held in the arms of my heavenly Father. In my deep need, I wished with all my heart that this fine young man might stay in my home and care for me like that forever. Alas, that was simply my selfishness at work.

However, Jesus did remain in my home for a few more years. How quickly those years passed. Already a fine carpenter, he took over Joseph's carpentry business, training up his brothers so that they could take over in time. He stepped easily into the role of provider and father figure to his siblings. Not that they always appreciated this or respected his wisdom and grace in dealing with them. But they could not have asked for better. Nor could I.

"Why do not you take a wife, Jesus?" my oldest daughter, Hannah, asked him one day as he was at work. I paused near his workbench, pretending to examine a small stool he had just finished, as I listened to his response.

He planed a piece of wood, going over it again and again until the plank was as smooth as the Sea of Galilee on a day without wind. "I already have my hands full with this family," he told her with a smile.

"But you should have a family of your own," she insisted. "There are lots of nice girls in Nazareth who think that Jesus the carpenter is a very good catch."

He laughed. "You better tell them to cast their nets elsewhere, little sister."

I suppose I was relieved that Jesus showed no interest in marriage. Although, Hannah was right. There were plenty of young women in our village who thought highly of my son, plenty who would have been pleased to marry the honest, hard-working carpenter who took such good care of his family.

Then suddenly everything changed. It happened when Jesus was around thirty years old. One morning, after seeing my firstborn son nearly every single day of his entire life, he bid me farewell, and, instead of going off to work, he simply walked away.

Something about the determined look in his eye reminded me of the time he had stayed in the temple to attend to his Father's business. I also knew, thanks to rumors that flew through our region like grassfire, that my dear cousin Elizabeth's son (who was nearly the same age as Jesus) had just started a very unusual sort of ministry. People were calling him John the Baptist and John the Preacher, and some even thought he might be the Messiah. Although, I also heard that he quickly set them straight on this account, assuring everyone with ears to hear that he was only getting them ready for the one who would soon come.

He told his listeners that while he, John, baptized with water, the one who was coming would baptize with fire. I am still uncertain as to what this means, for I have yet to see my son, the true Messiah, bring down fire on anyone. And, of course, now it seems too late. Even so, I hate to doubt John's prediction.

Naturally, I suspected that Jesus was

going off to listen to his cousin's preaching. And I later learned through a neighbor named Myra (she and her husband had witnessed this strange event for themselves) that Jesus had actually asked John to baptize him.

"John the mighty preacher was nearly speechless," Myra told me. "But then he said—and I swear that I am not making this up—that he was not worthy to tie Jesus's sandals and that Jesus should be the one doing the baptizing."

In that moment, I felt something running through me—a rush of excitement mixed with a very real fear. And I knew this was the beginning. Although I felt disappointed, I was not very surprised when Jesus did not come home that day. Myra told me that after the baptism Jesus had turned and walked away, still dripping, heading straight for the wilderness.

"I heard that John the Preacher lives in the wilderness," she said, probably to reassure me, "and that he survives on locusts and honey." She made a face. "Do you think your son is going to do the same?"

"Jehovah will watch over him," I told her, concealing my concerns from her curious eyes. "He will be fine."

For how could the mighty Jehovah allow any harm to come to his beloved Son? I remembered the times when I had fretted about something and Joseph had jokingly reminded me that God in his glory was perfectly able to send down legions of angels if necessary to protect young Jesus. And so I told myself that I need not worry as Jesus set out on his Messiah's mission. Jehovah would watch over him then as well.

But where was Jehovah yesterday? What was he doing when the sky turned dark and my son cried out for deliverance? Where was God then?

9

The next time I saw my son, after he had been baptized by his cousin, he was not the same man who had walked away from Nazareth only a week before. He had a different look in his eyes. Maybe it was some sort of spiritual confidence or just pure determination, but he had definitely changed. Now, he was as kind and loving and gracious as ever when he greeted his family, but it was obvious to me that his mission here on earth had begun.

It was not long before Jesus began to teach. But his teaching was unlike anything any of us had ever heard before. And the way he could speak with such conviction and hold the attention of his listeners was truly incredible. It was as if we could not get enough of his words. Even I, his own mother, was often caught as if spellbound by his ability to speak what I knew must be truth in a completely new and profound way. Truly amazing!

And yet he was my son. I had given birth to this young man, had nourished him from my own breast, had washed, fed, and cared for him when he was too little to care for himself. And yet he was God. It was almost too much for me to contain in my small, earthly head. But my heart knew it was true.

Not long after Jesus began his ministry, my favorite sister, Sarah, who lived in the neighboring town of Cana, invited us to visit her family and celebrate the wedding of her firstborn son. Her handsome Benjamin had been betrothed to a young woman from a fairly well-to-do family, and I am sure Sarah wanted to impress us with this match. Since I have always loved Benjamin, I was happy to go, as were my children. Even Jesus promised to meet up with us there. By now he had several faithful friends who traveled everywhere with him, soaking in all the words of his teaching as well as helping see to his needs. It was plain that my son was in good hands. Not only Jehovah's but also those of these loyal men who clearly loved their leader.

We all know that weddings do not come cheap, but it was obvious that Sarah and her husband had spent a lot on this one. However, they had no idea how many guests the wife's family would invite, and early in the evening poor Sarah realized they had completely run out of wine.

"Mary," she whispered to me. "Whatever are we going to do? We will appear to be the most thoughtless of all hosts, and poor Benjamin will be shamed in front of his new in-laws."

Feeling my sister's pain almost as my own, I sought out Jesus. I am not even sure why—for what did I really think he could do about it? But if Joseph had been alive, I am sure I would have run to him for help in just the same way.

"Jesus!" I used my most urgent tone to address my son. "They are out of wine, and Sarah is humiliated. Is there anything you can do?"

I will never forget the way he looked at me. Almost as if I was not really his mother. "This is not our problem," he told me with an authority that was slightly intimidating. "My time has not come yet. Do not push me, woman."

Well, for my firstborn son to address me in such a manner was rather shocking. Not that it was rude, for I have heard other grown men use the same terms with their mothers. But it felt so impersonal, as if he was gently but firmly shoving me away from him. For some reason—almost as if some other force was at work within me— I went ahead and told the servants to go and do whatever Jesus instructed them. To this day, I wonder at my nerve, but I can only attribute it to the mighty Jehovah.

Feeling nervous but expectant, I stood nearby and watched as Jesus told the servants to fetch the large water cisterns (there were six of them altogether, and each could hold nearly thirty gallons), and then he said to fill them to the brims with water. Without questioning, the servants obeyed.

After the water cisterns were full, Jesus told the servants to dip their wine jugs into these large vats and serve the wedding guests. Well, you could tell that the servants thought this was questionable behavior, but, for some reason, they did it anyway. Perhaps Jehovah was at work in them as well.

You should have seen those servants' faces—my face too, for that matter—when they poured out the water that had been miraculously changed into wine. And not just any ordinary wine, but the finest wine any of us had ever tasted.

"Why has the groom saved the best wine for last?" the bride's father demanded as he held up a cup and sniffed its bouquet. "This is much better than that cheap stuff you were serving us earlier."

Sarah looked at me with surprised but grateful eyes, and the wedding celebration continued late into the night and on into the next day. Was I amazed by the incredible miracle my son had performed? Well, of course; who would not be? But the main thing that kept me awake that night was the stinging memory of the way Jesus had looked at me, the way he had called me "woman" instead of "Mother." Almost as if he were dismissing me altogether, as if I was no longer his mother and someone worthy of respect and honor. And that is when I knew—I knew to the depths of my soul—something between us had changed. Something was separating us, like an invisible wedge that would go deeper and deeper, slowly driving us apart. And I believe that wedge was the Lord God Almighty. I was not sure why he would do this to me.

It became clearer to me, as time passed and Jesus's ministry and followers increased, that Jehovah, more than ever before, was truly manifest in this man. Jesus was not only the Son of God, but he and God were connected somehow—they were *one.* I began to realize that when you looked upon my son, you were looking upon the Lord God. Indeed, Jehovah had come to live and dwell among us in the form of Jesus. But as a mother who felt she was losing her firstborn son, this was a bitter taste of things to come.

Perhaps this was even the first slice of Simeon's prophecy, the sword that would pierce my soul, for I loved Jesus as much as—no, more than—ever. I loved him with a love that was fierce and perhaps even somewhat protective. As if I, a mere earthly woman, might somehow protect the mighty Jehovah. But I believe I still thought this. And God in his gracious glory was determined to put me in my proper place. And so he did. So he did.

My other children were quite stunned by what was happening with their eldest brother. Repeatedly they asked me how this was even possible. How had their own flesh-and-blood brother lived among them and then suddenly transformed himself into the Messiah? Their doubt and skepticism was written all over their faces, and my answers never seemed to satisfy them. Even when I quoted to them from the old prophets, such as Ezekiel and Isaiah (predictions of the Messiah Joseph had taught me back when we lived in

107

Egypt and had time for such long discussions), still they were unconvinced.

My sons were particularly skeptical of their brother's ministry. And one day, James, Joses, and Judas drew me into their concerns. Simon, the youngest, wisely remained silent.

"I have heard that some people think Jesus is crazy," James said.

"That is right," Joses agreed. "There is talk that he lives like an animal, that he does not take care of himself and thinks nothing of breaking the Sabbath."

"And some even say he teaches cannibalism," James said, "that he tells his followers they must eat his flesh and drink his blood."

I shuddered but said nothing.

"He is in great danger," Judas said, as if he was actually concerned for his half brother's welfare. "He is very close to going over the edge, Mother."

"We should go to him," James urged. "We should warn him to be more careful."

"And to take care of himself," Joses added. "Perhaps he needs a rest."

Their words were like thorns caught in

my clothing that day; they poked and stabbed at me until I was nearly sick with worry for Jesus. That was how I let my sons talk me into going to Galilee to see him.

"You are his mother," James said as we set out on our mission to rescue my first-born son. "Jesus must listen to you."

"We can talk him into coming home for a while," Joses said. "He needs to take a break from all his traveling and speaking."

I could tell they were concerned for Jesus, and I knew they really loved him. But something about our trip did not feel right. Even so, I could not quite put my finger on it. And their words combined with their strength of unity were persuasive.

It was not difficult to locate Jesus once we reached the small town in Galilee. We simply followed the crowd. They were clustered around a house where we were informed that Jesus was inside, reportedly teaching his disciples and others. But I remained outside as I asked one of Jesus's followers to go in and get him.

"Please tell Jesus that his mother and brothers are here to see him," I said in a voice filled with maternal authority. And my three other sons stood behind me, nodding. As I waited I tried to decide what I would say to Jesus. I thought he should be aware of our concern and listen to our warning. Perhaps he would even agree to come home.

But we waited and waited, and Jesus did not come out. Finally the man I had spoken to earlier emerged, but his face bore a frown.

"Where is my son?" I demanded, feeling slightly aggravated by our long wait in the noonday sun.

"Jesus has sent you a message," the man said.

"What is it?"

This poor man looked clearly uncomfortable with what he was about to say. First he shuffled his feet, then he cleared his throat, and finally he spoke. "Jesus said, 'Who is my mother? Who are my brothers?' "

"What?" James demanded. "He knows who we are—"

The man held up his hand to stop him. "Jesus also said that whoever does the will of his Father in heaven—those people are his mothers and brothers and sisters."

In other words, my eldest son had absolutely no interest in seeing his own family. It was as if we were strangers to him. Or worse, since he was continually surrounded by virtual strangers, we were even lower than that in his eyes. Or so it seemed.

So, there you see, Jehovah *did* put me in my place. Thoroughly humbled by my son's lack of reception, I turned away and began to walk toward home. But my sons were incensed that their own flesh and blood should treat them, and particularly me, in such a fashion. I was not paying close attention to their angry words. I was too caught up in a grief all my own, but I could tell by their tone of righteous indignation that they talked of little else for quite some time.

As I walked toward Nazareth, I felt that Jehovah was speaking to my heart, gently correcting me in regard to my eldest son—or rather the reaction I felt toward my son. Feeling the burning conviction of God's Spirit, I walked along in quiet repentance, my head bowed as I silently confessed my sin to Jehovah.

My sin, I knew, was my motherly pride. I actually felt that I was somehow responsible, if only in a small way, for Jesus's successful ministry—as if I should receive some kind of glory or honor. How it pains me even now to remember how I honestly believed this back then. What a silly, shallow woman I was! I still wonder sometimes why Jehovah chose someone like me to be the mother of his Son. I am so unworthy.

But I was not stupid, and I fully realized in that moment how pride truly does precede the fall. And so, for the sake of Jesus even more than for myself, I had no desire to stumble just then. I knew I had a responsibility to keep a pure heart not only before the Lord Jehovah, my God, but also before my son, the Holy One of Israel. And with this realization, I had tears of contrition streaming down both cheeks. So much so that I was unable to see clearly and finally had to stop walking. Along the side of the road, I stood and

sobbed, looking to the heavens and longing for forgiveness.

My sons, unaware of my heartache,
were quite a ways ahead before they noticed that I was no longer walking with
them.

"See!" James said as the three of them
hurried back to my side. Then he used the
edge of my veil to tenderly dab my wet
cheeks. "Jesus is a disrespectful son! He
has hurt our mother."

"He is tearing this family apart!" Joses
exclaimed. "Something should be done
about it."

I stopped crying, and, standing up
straight, I looked at the three of them. I en-
deavored to give all of them my sternest
expression, something I had always re-
served for only the worst of childhood of-
fenses but had not needed to use for
years.

"Quiet!" I finally said in a loud voice. "Be
silent, my sons."

They looked surprised, but, seeing that
I had attained their attention, I continued
in a quiet but very intense voice. "I cannot
force you to believe that your brother truly

is God's own Son or persuade you to accept him as the real Messiah, but I will *not* abide your slander of him for one more moment. Do you understand?"

Apparently they did, for they remained quite somber for the rest of the journey home. As I walked I continued silently praying to Jehovah. I thanked him for his correction on my soul, and I asked him to show all my children the truth about their eldest brother, to help them accept that the Lord God Almighty had ordained this event since the beginning of time and that no amount of skepticism or complaining could alter that fact.

From time to time I have noticed small things, like a nod of understanding from my oldest daughter, Hannah, or maybe I will catch Joses actually quoting his oldest brother—these little things give me a glimmer of hope for Jesus's siblings. But, for the most part, my grown children, like the majority of my neighbors in Nazareth, are about as faithful as a millstone when it comes to accepting Jesus as Messiah.

Still, I cannot help but wonder what they are thinking now. I am sure my children have received word of their brother's tragic death, since they are still here for Passover and all of Jerusalem hums with the news. Are they sorry they did not treat him better during his last years on earth? Do they wish they had done things differently?

This weary mother's heart cannot even begin to figure out such things on the second sorrowful day of our great loss. And I have long since learned there is nothing I can do about such things anyway. So once again—as I have done so many times before—I will pray. I will place my other children in God's hands. Only Jehovah can convince them of the truth.

10

Most of my pride was put to death on the road home from Galilee that day. Now, I am not perfect, and I still have my moments when I must remind myself that I am only an earthen vessel—and not a very lovely one, at that. But something inside me was greatly changed that day. As a result, I kept a distance from my son's ministry for quite a while. It seemed the right thing to do at the time. Perhaps it was Jehovah's spirit guiding me—that still, small voice I have come to respect and love. But I knew I should stay away for a spell. And so I did.

Even so, I would ask anyone who had

seen him to tell me everything they could remember. "What did he say?" I would inquire eagerly. "What did he teach?" And it was during this time when I felt myself becoming like a child who was hungry for truth and knowledge. And after what seemed a long period of waiting, I finally knew that the time had come. I was ready. Ready to go and sit among the hundreds of others, just another believing face in the crowd, eager to hear and learn from my Lord. For that is how I had begun to think of him—as my Lord. And this renaming of my son brought great peace and comfort to my heart. Indeed, things were changing in me!

How my spirit rejoiced on the day I felt that still, small voice telling me that it was time—that I was free to go and hear him. I already knew that Jesus was up near the Sea of Galilee, and I quickly packed a few things and set out on the road. As I traveled I met others who were going to hear him as well. People from as far away as Jerusalem had heard about his teachings. Many had left jobs and even families to journey up here just to see him.

"How long have you known of Jesus?" a young woman about the age of my Hannah asked me.

"I am still just getting to know my Lord," I told her. And this was not necessarily untrue.

"Have you heard that he can heal the sick?" another woman asked.

I simply nodded and listened as my fellow travelers spoke of the marvelous things Jesus had done. Without revealing my relationship to Jesus, I took in their comments, hiding each word like a tender morsel in my heart. Then I stopped in Cana to visit my sister Sarah, who had been recently widowed. I talked with her awhile, expressing my sorrow at her loss. Then I told her where I was going, and Sarah, still amazed at the wine miracle, decided she would join me on this pilgrimage. I was surprised but truly happy to have her company. Even so, I did ask her not to reveal our identity to those we traveled with, and she agreed.

"It is much simpler this way," I explained.

"But you should be proud of your son,

Mary," she said as we walked a short ways behind the rest of the crowd.

"It is complicated," I tried to explain. "He is no ordinary son."

"Well, I always knew he was very special," she said. I had to smile to myself at this, since I think Sarah, like most of our family and neighbors, never suspected there was anything very unusual about Jesus before his ministry began.

"And he has always loved his aunt Sarah," I told her.

"Can you believe we are doing this?" she said in a tone of voice that reminded me of when we were both girls, journeying to Jerusalem for Passover. "I am so thankful that our children are grown and married. It is wonderful to have this freedom to be able to go and see him."

I had to agree with her. There was something very invigorating about being out on the road on a fine summer day, traveling with others who were excited about hearing the powerful words of Jesus. I could hear bits of conversations. Some said, "He is the new king, come to deliver us." Others still thought he was a prophet. Some were unsure but curious to see him for themselves.

"This is so exciting!" Sarah said as we entered Capernaum, the place where we had heard Jesus was staying. And it was exhilarating. A sense of energy filled the air, similar to the power you experience during a lightning storm, only not as frightening. People were everywhere, filling the streets and every open space. Young people, old people, sick people, and lots of children. All had left their homes, some coming from as far off as Gaza, to descend upon this small fishing town to hear Jesus teach. It was unlike anything I had ever seen before.

The next morning Sarah and I sat mesmerized among the hordes of listeners as Jesus preached from a high position situated on the crest of a small mountain. And, truly, it was as if the Lord God Jehovah himself was speaking—Jesus's words were that powerful and that profound! Perhaps what touched me most the first time I sat and listened to him speak was when he gave what I later considered the "Blessed" sermon. Of course, I know his words are for everyone, but somehow I felt he was speaking directly to me that day. His promises were like a soothing balm for my aching heart.

"Blessed are you when you realize
    you are spiritually impoverished,
    for you will have the kingdom of
    heaven.
Blessed are you when you mourn,
    for you shall receive comfort.
Blessed are you when you are
    humble and meek,
    for you shall inherit the earth.
Blessed are you when you hunger
    and thirst for righteousness,
    for you will be satisfied.
Blessed are you when you show
    mercy,
    for you will be shown mercy.
Blessed are you when your heart is
    pure,
    for you shall see God.
Blessed are you when you make
    peace,
    for you will be called God's own
    children.

Blessed are you when you are
persecuted for my sake,
for the kingdom of heaven will be
yours."

And on and on he continued throughout the day. Now, if he had been a mere man, or even just a prophet, I imagine the crowd would have thinned eventually. People would have tired of listening and simply gone home or in pursuit of some other diversion. But as the day progressed, the crowd only grew larger and larger, until there must have been thousands.

"He is astonishing," said a woman to my right. "He must truly be the Son of God."

I nodded, then turned my eyes back to Jesus. But for a brief moment I felt a ripple of fear running through my soul. Was that *pride* I was experiencing as I watched my son preaching? I had so hoped to be done with that by now. But, upon more careful examination, I realized that it was only a feeling of awe—just pure and simple awe. His words were that inspiring!

Even as I wait here, knowing that his lifeless body lies in the tomb, I am still inspired by his words. His death does not change the truth he spoke. I only wish I could understand why Jehovah has allowed him to be silenced like this. To me, it seems all wrong. But then I am not the one who controls the universe. I know I must trust Jehovah in his wisdom. I must believe that good will arise out of evil. *Please, God, help my unbelief.*

I glance around the room where we are still gathered. There is some comfort in not being alone on this dark day, and I can see that others are struggling in their spirits, perhaps even more than I. This has been a very long day for everyone. God, in his mercy, has shrouded the sunlight for most of the day. But I can tell by the dusky light now filtering through the clouds on the western horizon that this second day of waiting is drawing to an end. I do not know what we thought might happen here today. But I can tell that discouragement is growing with the darkness.

Simon Peter seems the most lost. His eyes are draped in sadness, and this usually robust and fiery fisherman appears broken and weary and very old today. John told me earlier that Peter is grieving deeply, not only over the loss of his Lord, but also for the fact that he denied knowing Jesus three times yesterday.

"But Jesus told him it would happen just that way," John explained to me in a hushed voice. "Peter should not be so hard on himself."

I nodded. "I think we are all examining our hearts right now."

I knew there were no words I could say to Peter, nothing I could do to ease his pain. But I paused on my way going outside, and, placing my hand on one of his broad shoulders, I looked directly into his eyes. I wanted to tell him that he must know that Jesus has already forgiven him. How could Jesus, the one who taught us so much about forgiveness, not forgive his dear friend? But I also knew that, in the same way a fisherman shakes off the spray from the sea, Peter would only shake off my words. Even so, I hope the look in my eyes conveyed my son's mercy to him.

I remember the first time I met Simon Peter. Jesus had already gathered a dozen good men who had left jobs and homes and families to remain by his side. And I knew that these men were my son's closest and dearest friends. Almost always with him, they heard much more of Jesus's teachings than the rest of us. I was later told that the purpose of their intense training was to enable them to go out and spread the good news to others.

I am not sure what will happen now. How can they go out and tell people how God's Son said and did so many miraculous things and then tell them he was killed? It does not seem a good ending for this story. And I know his disciples are frustrated.

When I first met Jesus's new friends, I was somewhat surprised that they seemed such ordinary men. I do not know, I suppose I expected to see some priests or more highly educated or influential men in the bunch. But then I was reminded of how Jehovah works and the way he reveals himself to the lowly. Why, is not that exactly how he chose me, and even my dear Joseph? And so, as I got to know these men, I could see why my son picked them for his most intimate friends. They are honest men with good hearts, and I think that any one of them would have laid down his life for my son. Of course, he would not allow that. Even when Peter attempted to defend Jesus at the time of his arrest, Jesus put a stop to it.

"There was a lot going on at once," John told me. "But in the scuffle, Peter grabbed a sword and sliced off the ear of the high priest's servant."

"Oh!" I glanced over to where Peter was sitting with his face to the wall. I knew how committed to my son he was, and I could believe he would do something that violent if he thought it would help matters. Poor Peter.

"Jesus told us that everyone who takes up the sword will perish by the sword," John continued. "And then he healed the servant's ear just as good as new."

I nodded. Yes, I could imagine my son doing that. He had such a compassionate heart when it came to suffering. I vaguely wonder how many people he has healed during these past three years. It was almost a daily thing—and it was not unusual for many to be healed at one time. I still feel a sense of wonder to consider all the miracles Jesus has done, but in some ways I think we all simply came to accept such actions as perfectly normal. I am sure that we actually began to expect the miracles—perhaps we even took them for granted.

I bow my head now and remind myself that I must never take any of this for granted. I must never allow myself to think that what happened here, Jesus's ministry and his teaching and miracles, was not a big deal. Indeed, it was a very big deal. And, I suspect, it is not finished yet.

11

The women, led by Mary of Magdala, are serving dinner now. I offered to help, but once again they told me not to bother myself. I try not to look too uncomfortable as they wait on me. But I do remember Jesus's teachings on servants. He said that we all need to serve each other, and I have always been most happy to serve. Indeed, it is much more pleasing to me to serve than to be served. But this is not a day of comfort.

I watch Mary's face as she serves. Such sadness! I know she loved my son wholeheartedly. And everyone knows she is a woman with deep passion and strong feelings. Some say she wears her heart on her sleeve, but I think they simply do not understand the complexity of this woman.

I still remember the first time I met her. It was not long after my son delivered her from some very disturbing spirits that had plagued her for years. Some call them demons; some call them unclean spirits. I am no expert on such things, but I do wonder if Mary's tender heart didn't place her in a position to be victimized by such things. For once you know her, you can see that she is a woman of intense emotions. Like an artist or a poet, she sees and experiences life on a level some of us can only imagine. And so it is my personal belief that these strong emotions and compulsions could easily overpower her to the point where she lost control of her life. Fortunately for her, that is when Jesus came along and drove them out of her.

"I can never repay your son for what he has done for me," she told me when she discovered I was Jesus's mother.

I nodded. "None of us can."

"Even you?" she said, her beautiful dark eyes opened wide in surprise.

I smiled. "Even me."

"I have decided to devote my entire life to him," she told me.

"As have I."

Then she took my hand in hers and squeezed it. "Then we are like sisters."

"Sisters in our Lord."

"Mary and Mary."

And so we have been like sisters. I have loved this woman from the beginning. Of course, I must admit that I was a little intimidated by her at first, for it was plain to see, by her expensive clothing and refined speech, that she was a woman of considerable means. But when I looked into her eyes, I saw gentleness and mercy there. I saw wisdom and understanding—the kind that is conceived out of great pain. And I loved her even more.

If Jesus were just an ordinary man and not the Son of God, Mary of Magdala is exactly the sort of woman I would have wished to become my daughter-in-law. She has the kind of intelligence and depth of spirit I admire. Even as I watch her serving here today, a woman who comes from a wealthy home where she is used to being served and waited upon, I see her humility of spirit, her thoughtful ways, and I am inspired.

I know she loved my son deeply, and I think there was even a time when she was *in love* with my son in the same way that I was in love with my Joseph. But, to be fair, we were all in love with Jesus. How could we not be? To look in his eyes was to see God the Father. His presence alone brought comfort, grace, healing, mercy . . . to know him was simply to love him. And then, of course, some have the capacity to love more than others.

But Jesus never took advantage of Mary's passionate love for him, not in the way a human man would. And even as he allowed the various women to minister to his needs, he always maintained his position as teacher and Lord. There was never any misunderstanding in that regard. And I must respect Mary for this. She is an honorable woman. And, in some ways, she even reminds me of my cousin Elizabeth.

Dear, dear Elizabeth. I was so saddened to hear of her death several years ago. Of course, she was quite elderly and was preceded in death by her husband, Zacharias. But I felt bad that she passed on before actually seeing the incredible ministry of both of our sons. How she would have rejoiced to learn of how her son baptized my son down in the Jordan River!

However, my regrets quickly turned into thankfulness when I heard of the vicious murder of her son John. No mother should be forced to witness such spiteful brutality, not even from a distance. Even now I shudder to remember the story. But, in light of what has happened to my own son, I force myself to consider John's execution once more. My young cousin's troubles began when he rightly accused Herod, our supposed leader, for having taken his brother's wife, Herodias, as his own.

This public statement landed poor John in prison. Then, during a birthday celebration when Herod reportedly became drunk with mixed wines, Herodias's daughter performed some kind of erotic dance that pleased the inebriated Herod. So much so that he offered to give her whatever she desired. And that was when the woman requested that he give her John the Baptist's head on a platter. Her request was granted, and John was beheaded.

I remember questioning Jehovah at the time, wondering how he allowed such wickedness not only in this world but in positions of Jewish leadership. But then I was reminded that the Lord God Jehovah does not control the will of man. And the will of man, much of the time, seems determined to turn its back on God and to pursue its own selfish ways.

Of course, Jesus exhorted us again and again to turn back to God the Father. And many of us had been doing just that—through Jesus, who was like a door, a gate that took us right to Jehovah. But now our door is gone. How will we enter?

Our meal is ending now, but I see there is nearly as much food on the table as when we began. No one has much of an appetite. And no one has much to say. I move to my place by the window as the women begin to clear away the food. The sky is dark now, and another hopeless night looms before us. *How long must we wait, Lord?*

"Let us remember and be encouraged by what our Lord told us," John says, and the room suddenly grows very quiet. "On his last evening with us, our Master said, 'No man has a greater love than to lay down his life for his friends.' "

The women stop clearing the table, and we all focus our attention on John, waiting for him to continue, hoping he might also have the words of life that we all dearly miss.

"And then Jesus said, 'You are my friends if you do as I instruct you. I do not call you servants anymore. For a servant is unaware of what his master is up to. But I am calling you friends because I have told you all that my Father has told me.' "

I can tell that the others are feeling more hopeful, thinking that perhaps John is remembering something vitally important, or maybe Jesus is speaking through him, and maybe something he says tonight will make sense out of what feels like a bad mistake.

"Go on," John's brother James urges.

"Our Lord said that we did not choose him, but that he chose us. Not only did he choose us, but he *appointed* us."

Heads are nodding now. The flicker of hope and memory is burning brighter.

"Jesus said," John continues, " 'I appointed you so that you could bear fruit and that your fruit should remain. And if you ask the Father for anything in my name, he will give it to you.' "

"But what does that mean?" Andrew asks.

"Explain it to us," James insists. "Because I *have* been asking the Father to do something. And I have been asking in Jesus's name. And yet it does not happen."

"We need to have faith," John says. "Even if it looks hopeless."

"I just want him to come back," Mary of Magdala says in a desperate voice. Then she staggers slightly, as if she is about to faint, and one of the other women helps her sit down. Once seated, Mary takes her head into her hands and weeps like a brokenhearted child. Soon many of us are weeping. We cannot help it. I look to John with tears blurring my eyes. I appreciate his words and his willingness to encourage our hearts, but now I see that he too is crying.

I wonder how much grief we can endure and whether hope will ever live again. I turn my face to look out the window now. The world is dark, but I can see the golden glow of lamplights flickering in the windows in the homes down below. I am reminded of when Jesus said that we, his followers, were to be like a city on a high hill, something people could spot from miles away—or like a lamp set upon a pedestal, shedding its light for all to see.

But it seems our lamp is burning low tonight, or perhaps the evil one has placed a bushel basket over it to obscure its light completely. For if anyone is watching us, Jesus's devoted followers, all they would see tonight is a sad little group of lost and confused children hovering in the darkness. Not very impressive.

I remember the prayer that Jesus taught us. It is one I have repeated often, but not since my son's death. I look out over Jerusalem now—the city that killed my son—

and I quietly whisper the words into the night air.

"My Father in heaven.
Holy is your name.
May your kingdom come to us,
    and may your will be fulfilled here
    on earth,
    even as it is fulfilled in heaven.
Give us what we need for this day.
And forgive us our sins,
    as we forgive those who sin
    against us.
And lead us away from temptation,
    and deliver us from evil.
For your kingdom is powerful and
    glorious for all eternity.
Amen."

To my surprise, I feel a bit better now. I consider the words of this prayer, and I wonder if I have ever completely understood the meaning before. Or even if I understand it now. But I do believe God's kingdom came to us—it came to earth in the sinless form of my son, the Lord Jesus. And yet it still does not seem that

God's will has been fulfilled here on earth. If anything, it seems that it was thwarted when Jesus was killed yesterday. And I do not understand the purpose in this. Still, I trust Jehovah and I trust Jesus, and I do believe God's kingdom is forever. And so we must continue to wait.

I decide that I will attempt to encourage myself, following John's example, by remembering the words Jesus spoke during his ministry. I will see how many of his words I can recall. Remembering how I have planted them like seeds in my heart, I will see if they are still there. Perhaps my tears have watered them recently, and maybe they will finally begin to grow. Or at least they will help me pass the time until morning. And then what? What will I do tomorrow?

"Do not worry about tomorrow," my son once told us. "For tomorrow has enough worries for itself." Well, that is true enough. And I cannot even count the times I have cheered myself with what he said next. I suppose it was the gardener in me that latched onto these happy words.

"Think about the flowers on the hillside," he said as he held up a glorious red anemone flower. "They do not worry about how to spin or how to weave fine cloth. They never fret over what they will wear. Yet even King Solomon, in all his glory days, never turned out as beautifully dressed as these pretty flowers."

I remember how I laughed the first time I heard him say that. How perfectly appropriate. And how easy to remember. His stories were like that for me. He made a very clear point, but not with fancy words. He simply painted word pictures and told us stories we could remember. Parables we could repeat to one another as we traveled the roads of life. And now I am hoping his stories and my memories can carry me through another night.

12

As the women gather up the remains of our mostly untouched supper, I am reminded of another time when there was a surplus of leftovers. It happened near Capernaum shortly after the execution of John the Baptist. I am sure Jesus was grieving the death of his cousin. Probably on several levels.

I had heard rumors that some of John's followers had turned to Jesus, hailing him as king but pressuring him to take his kingdom by force. Many of our people were tired of being oppressed by not only the Romans but also the crooked leadership of our own people. As a result, people hungry for a leader, a prophet—yes, even the Messiah—came from all over, clamoring to see Jesus.

Sarah and I had just returned from Cana, where we had spent a few days with her family, but hearing of John's death disturbed us greatly. We both suddenly longed to be near Jesus once more. And we were not alone. We overheard one man estimating that there were at least five thousand men present that day. And that combined with women and children could probably be four times that number. Incredible.

Jesus and his disciples had taken a boat across the lake. I later learned this was simply to escape the huge crowd of people. Of course, the people had no idea, and they simply walked around the lake to the place where they had heard the Master would be teaching later in the day. Naturally, and not unlike sheep, Sarah and I went with them.

We all ended up at a lovely, albeit somewhat remote, area on the north side of the lake. A slight breeze cooled the afternoon air, and before long we found places to sit on the hillside, waiting for our Lord to arrive.

I could tell, even from a distance, that Jesus was tired and, I am sure, overwhelmed by John's death and the subsequent pressure from John's disciples. But, making the boat into his platform, he stood before the crowd and taught just the same. That is how compassionate this man was. He always put the needs of others above his own. And although he was weary and grieving, his teaching that day (at least for me) was some of his best and most memorable. Perhaps that is because he spoke of plants and seeds and growing things, subjects that were near and dear to my heart. And I suppose I even wondered if my love of gardens had somehow had an effect on him. Although, as Jehovah is my witness, I take no credit for his sermon. Besides, it was plain to see that Jesus's heavenly Father was speaking directly through him.

"A man went out to plant seeds." Jesus began with these simple words, and the crowd grew instantly quiet as his voice carried across the water and up the hillside. "And as he was planting, some of the seeds fell along the road and were immediately gobbled up by the birds. And some seeds fell into the rocky places where the soil was not good, causing these seeds to spring up quickly, but when the sun came out, the plants became scorched and withered. Then some of the seeds fell among the thorns, and the thorns took over and choked them out."

I remember feeling a bit worried, wondering what kind of farmer would be so careless with precious seeds? I could not imagine where Jesus was going with this story.

Then he continued. "But the other seeds fell onto good soil, producing a good crop, some a hundredfold, some sixty, some thirty." Then he paused for a moment before he called out, "He who has ears to hear, let him hear!"

Well, I was not exactly sure what his story meant, but I did have hungry ears, and I wanted to be able to understand the meaning. But why did it always seem to be hidden? I glanced at Sarah, curious as to whether she understood the meaning, but she looked as confused as I felt. In fact, I noticed that everyone did.

I later learned the meaning of this parable from Simon Peter. He told me the disciples had been puzzled too, but Jesus had explained it all later. "The seeds are like Jesus's words, words that tell of God's kingdom," Peter told me.

I nodded eagerly. "And we, the listeners, are like the different kinds of soil?"

"That is right. Some of us are like the road—our soil is packed so hard and tight that the words just bounce right off and are easily taken from us."

"Yes, I have been like that before," I admitted.

"So have I. And I think that is also a good description of some of the scribes and Pharisees—their soil is packed hard as a stone."

"Maybe so."

"And some of us are like the rocky soil," he continued. "We get excited about the kingdom words, so the seeds spring up quickly, but we do not have the right kind of soil to grow the roots we need. And when the sun gets hot, we wither." He lowered his voice and said, "I think Jesus was talking about some of John's followers, the ones who are urging him to take his kingdom by force. But Jesus does not want to do it that way.

"And, finally, there is the good soil, and those are the hearts that are ready for the seeds. Those are the people who will grow good crops that yield many more seeds."

"That makes sense, Peter," I told him. "Thank you."

Peter looked troubled. "I see how you keep a distance from your son, Mary. And I have heard the things he has said to you—things that might hurt a mother's heart. But believe me, I know he loves you."

"Yes. I know he does too. But he is right in saying that those who do the Father's will are his mothers and brothers and sisters. And I respect that." I smiled. "You see, my son is also my Lord."

"He is my Lord too."

And later that same day, Peter had the opportunity to prove it. But that is another story.

All the things from supper have been cleared away now, and I remember back to that day when all the thousands listened to my son preaching from the boat down on the water. As the day drew to an end, it became clear that the crowds were hungry and that we were far from civilization. Like many of the others, Sarah and I had left our provisions in the home where we had been staying, and now it was suppertime and those provisions were several hours away.

Jesus's disciples told him he should send the crowds away so they could get food. But Jesus told his disciples they should feed the crowds. Well, I am sure this must have surprised them, since the only food they had was several loaves of bread and a couple of dried fish that had been donated by a generous little boy. But Jesus took these items and blessed them and broke them, telling his disciples to go out and feed the crowd. And so they did. To our amazement, there was plenty of bread and fish and everyone ate until they were full!

"This is like the wine at Benjamin's wedding!" Sarah exclaimed as she bit into another piece of fish.

"Have you ever tasted bread this delicious?" I asked.

And we ate as much as we wanted. But it was all those baskets full of leftover bread and fish that surprised me so. I think I heard that there were twelve all totaled. Miraculous!

But that was then. Everything is different now. I shift my position and glance over to where Simon Peter is slumped against the wall and appears to be sleeping, but I suspect he is actually wide awake. Poor man. How I wish he could forgive himself. Has he forgotten the words of his Lord?

I know he will never forget what happened later that same day, after they had fed the huge crowd. With full stomachs, the crowd began breaking up and people started heading back to town. Evening was approaching, and I remember feeling relieved to see that Jesus appeared to be leaving too, going off by himself. And I hoped it was to have a good rest.

Yes, I fully realized by then that he was

the Son of God and perfectly capable of taking care of himself as well as all of humanity, but, as his earthly mother, I still hoped he might get some much deserved peace and quiet, even if only for a short spell. His disciples, acting as his guards, would not allow any of the straggling listeners to follow as Jesus headed away from the lake. Soon everyone was back on their way to Capernaum and the disciples were getting back into their boat and preparing to row across the lake. Their plan, I learned later, was to meet up with Jesus on the other side sometime the following day.

We were almost back to town when the wind began to pick up and howl. It was obvious that a big storm was brewing, and Sarah and I began to walk faster. When we were nearly to town, we turned to look back at the lake, and that was when we noticed that the waves were cresting quite high.

"I hope his disciples will be okay out there," she said with concern.

In all honesty, I felt thankful to know that my son was safely on land, but I kept

149

these thoughts to myself as we hurried into town. We had just gotten safely into Sarah's sister-in-law's house when the wind began to wail and scream like demons from hell.

"Those unfortunate men," Sarah said as we shook the rain from our outer garments. "Can you imagine what it is like out there on the lake?"

Her sister-in-law frowned. "Well, if there is anyone on the lake right now, you probably will not be seeing those poor souls again. Who would be out in this?"

"Jesus's disciples," Sarah said sadly.

Then her sister-in-law reached for my arm. "Dear Mary, please tell me, is your son with them?"

"No," I assured her. "Jesus is safely on land."

As it turned out, I was wrong. Not only was Jesus not safely on land, he was out there in the middle of the storm, walking right on top of the water! I have never seen a man as excited as Simon Peter when he told me this remarkable story several days later.

"We thought we were goners," he said.

"That storm was trying to swallow up our boat for good." He shook his head. "Being a fisherman, I have seen some bad storms in my day, but that one was a monster." Then he went on to tell me how he had seen Jesus walking on the water toward them. "I could not believe it at first," he said. "I honestly thought I was imagining the whole thing. But then the others saw him too, and we knew it was real. He called out to us, telling us not to be afraid." Peter shook his head and laughed. "Then I said, 'Lord, if it is really you, tell me to come out to you on the water.' And Jesus said, 'Come.' "

By now Peter's brother Andrew had joined us. "Yes," Andrew said. "And brave Peter went out on the water—"

"I did!" Peter exclaimed. "I was really walking on the water—"

"Until he got scared and started to sink," Andrew teased.

"I did not see you out there walking on the water," Peter said. "At least I gave it a try."

"And lucky for you that Jesus rescued you."

"But that is when we all knew for sure, Mary," said Peter, more serious now. "We all got down on our knees, right there in the boat, and we all proclaimed your son as the Son of God."

"Thank you for telling me this," I told them. "It means so much to me."

I think it was at that time that I really began to believe that Jesus was invincible, that, no matter what happened, he could not be harmed or debilitated, and certainly not killed. But it seems I was wrong about that too.

13

I awaken from a horrible dream where cruel men are pounding heavy nails through my son's hands. Slamming their hammers again and again as blood splatters and Jesus winces in pain. Then, being only half awake, I am relieved to realize it was only a dream—a horrible nightmare. But my relief is short-lived when full consciousness and memory returns. And that is when I know—it really happened.

Now those vivid images of Jesus, bleeding and already in severe pain, being strapped down onto those rough wooden beams as men hold his beaten body in place so they can pound metal spikes through his hands and his feet, are freshly burned into my mind. The clanging of the hammer, metal upon metal, still rings in my ears.

Lord, help me, I pray with desperation. *Please, help me!* And suddenly, and thankfully, I hear the pounding of another hammer, wood upon wood this time, and another image comes to mind. I can see Jesus working in his father's workshop. His tall, lean frame is bent over as he carefully pounds a wooden peg into a lovely trunk that has been crafted with careful precision. I can almost smell the fragrant aroma of cedar shavings as I watch my Joseph smiling down on this fine young man, nodding with approval.

"You are a better craftsman than I," Joseph says to Jesus.

"Can a pupil be greater than his teacher?" Jesus asks his earthly father.

"Maybe if he has a good teacher." And they both laugh.

Those were happy days. Back when my Joseph was alive and our family lived together under one roof. But times changed. And there was that brief period when I truly believed I could never be happy again. It was after Joseph died and most of my children were married (some happily, some not), and then Jesus set out on his ministry, keeping me at arm's length. But after that period came to an end, and as I began to understand and accept my new position with Jesus, respecting him as my Lord, my life became very happy again.

Indeed, I think the past two years have been some of the happiest for me. No one was as surprised about this as I was. Shortly before my own mother died, just as my oldest children were becoming young adults, she told me how those later years, with her children now raised and waiting on her, were the best. "It is a time to play with the grandchildren," she told me. "Welcome it when it comes, Mary. It is one of the most blessed times of life." I only wish she could have lived longer to enjoy more years like that. But, heeding my mother's words, I was determined to take pleasure in this season of my life as well.

Having the freedom to travel with my

sister and hear the words of life that came from the mouth of God's own Son was much more rewarding than I ever imagined possible. Of course, the fly in the ointment was that my other children still did not understand or even accept it.

"Why do you go away so much, Mother?" Hannah complained to me one day. "Do you not want to watch your granddaughter growing up?"

"I love little Mary," I told her as I took the toddler into my lap. "And nothing pleases me more than seeing her grow."

"Then why do you leave all the time?" Hannah frowned.

"You know why I leave," I said as I braided Mary's dark curls. "I have told all of you that I feel there is much to learn from the Son of God."

"He is just Jesus, Mother."

"To you, he is just Jesus. To me and thousands of others, he is the Son of God, Messiah, and he has the words of life— words my spirit longs to hear." And then I told her the story of the man who had two sons. She and her younger sister listened intently as they worked together to grind grain into flour. I tried to tell the story as well as Jesus had. But when I was done, they both looked rather confused.

"That is not fair," Hannah said. "The older brother stayed home like a good son, helping his family and being responsible. But then the younger brother came home after spending his entire inheritance, and the father went out and welcomed him and even gave him the finest robe?"

"And then slaughtered the fatted calf?" my other daughter added.

Well, at least they were listening.

"And the younger son was just out having a good time," Hannah said.

"It did not sound like that good of a time," my younger daughter commented. "Eating with the pigs and all. But even so, Mother, I have to agree with Hannah. It does not seem fair to me either."

"But it was as if the father's son had been dead," I tried to explain. "Imagine if you thought one of your children was dead—and then he came back to you. How happy you would be!"

They both nodded now. Mothers can always understand this feeling.

"But what does it mean?" Hannah asked as she poured flour into a storage pot.

"Just that," I said. "Only you have to imagine the story being that of your heavenly Father. Think how Jehovah must rejoice when one of his children returns to him."

Hannah got a sly look on her face. "And think, dear Mother, how your children rejoice when you come home to them."

I just smiled. There is no way you can make people understand something they do not want to understand. And while I do not like thinking of my precious daughters as swine, I was not sure that it was wise for me to continue throwing these pearls out for them to trample upon. Although, I must admit that I did continue to do so occasionally, and I suspect I will probably continue doing so until the day I die. For I am, after all, a mother. Tell me, does a mother ever give up?

As I was saying, my children always seemed sad to see me leaving. But I could not help myself. Whenever I heard that Jesus was nearby, I felt I had wings attached to my feet, and I could not wait to fly. In some ways, I think my children were a bit envious of this newfound freedom of mine. I think they believed they should own a part of me, that they should be able to pin me down, to have me remain in their company whether I liked it or not.

"There she goes again," Hannah said as she balanced little Mary on one hip and sadly shook her head.

"Yes, there she goes," my other daughter said in a pained voice that sounded just a bit insincere. "I wonder when we will see her again."

"It will not be long," I promised as I waved and headed on my way.

"Tell Aunt Sarah hello," Hannah called with a slightly wistful tone.

But whenever I invited them to take a day trip with me when I knew that Jesus was teaching nearby, they quickly came up with excuses. I just do not understand that. I would think they would have been happy to escape their everyday chores for a little adventure on the road, not to mention some unforgettable teaching. But always they would say, "No, thank you, Mother. Not this time."

Even when I left my family to join Sarah during this Passover, explaining that she and I both felt the need to be near our Lord, still they could not accept this.

"But this is Passover," James complained. "It is time for families to be together, and you are our mother."

"Jesus is my family too," I told him. "Just as those who do the will of our heavenly Father are my family."

"Are you saying we are *not* your family?" James looked indignant.

I smiled at him. "You will always be my children, and I will always love you. But I cannot choose you over my heavenly Father."

And then I left to meet Sarah. She and I had already made plans to stay with some women friends who were close followers of Jesus—Joanna and Susanna and the other Marys along with a few more. These devoted women had committed themselves during the past two years to serving our Lord, and I was honored to be included among them. And although I do not like to hurt my children's feelings, the truth is that I do feel more related to those who believe in the Son of God than I do to my own flesh-and-blood relatives. I cannot deny it.

I think this was best driven home one time when Jesus came through our hometown for a brief visit. I remember the day vividly. I was so excited at the prospect of him sharing the good news among our neighbors and relatives in Nazareth. I had told many people, some who had already passed judgment based on hearsay, encouraging them that this was their chance to go and hear Jesus for themselves. Not only was I happy to see Jesus having this opportunity to convince the locals that his words were true, I was hopeful that he and his disciples would honor our home with a visit. I had spent days gathering foods to prepare a fine dinner for all of them.

"Listen to Jesus," I urged everyone who would listen. "See for yourself if his words are not the truth."

I was not too surprised, although I was

deeply dismayed, to see that my own family had little interest in hearing him teach.

"He is our brother," James said in an uninterested voice, as if that explained everything.

"Why should we leave our work just to hear *him* speak?" Joses asked.

But I did notice Joses and James as well as Simon hanging like dried cornhusks on the perimeters of the small crowd that had gathered at the synagogue to hear Jesus. And, as always, Jesus's teaching was excellent, and even the priests were impressed with his knowledge and skill. But suddenly—almost instantly—they seemed angered by that very thing, as if they resented that a local man could be so wise.

"Where did this *man* get this kind of wisdom?" a respected elder demanded. "How is he able to do mighty works?"

"Is not he just the carpenter's son?" another said. "Is not his mother Mary?"

"That is right," the elder said. "And are not his brothers and sisters ordinary people who live in our town? What makes him think he is so special?"

Soon they were all scoffing him and no one wanted to listen.

"A prophet is honored everywhere," Jesus said calmly, quoting old Scripture, "except in his hometown and in his own house."

The part about "his own house" hurt me a little. It made me sad to think Jesus did not feel honored in his family home, but then I knew it was true. Everyone in his immediate family, except me, refused to believe in him. They would not accept that he had been sent by God. And so he left Nazareth the same morning. Shaking the dust from his feet, I am sure, as he and his disciples continued on to places where crowds of thousands hungered for his words and thirsted for his miracles. He did not waste his time on our unbelieving and insignificant little town. And I do not blame him.

In fact, I felt a similar sense of rejection myself, as if I too was being dishonored— of course, my shunning was nothing like the way they treated Jesus, but it existed nonetheless. I would walk down to the well, and suddenly I would hear the voices get quieter, followed by hushed whispers and quick sideways glances. I knew what they were saying. And it hurt. Deeply.

It seemed the only real joy I found in my hometown was being in the privacy of my little garden. I loved taking my grandchildren there with me, teaching them to love and respect the plants. But one cannot hide in one's garden forever.

As a result, it became increasingly easier to leave my hometown and to travel with the crowds that followed Jesus's ministry. When Jesus said that foxes have holes and birds have nests but the Son of Man has nowhere to lay his head, I could almost understand. For sometimes it seemed I had no home either. Surely, I knew I still had my home back in Nazareth, the one so lovingly built for me by Joseph and now shared with two of my sons and their families, but more and more I did not feel at home there. Perhaps it was because I was thinking more about my heavenly home and my heavenly Father. Or perhaps it was simply because of my belief in the deity of my firstborn son, combined with the fact that I no longer felt welcome among my own neighbors.

But all these worries were instantly forgotten whenever I heard Jesus preach. Like so many others in the crowd, I devoured his words of life. I wanted to store them all inside of me so I could pull them out one by one later and at will. For the first time ever, I wished I was able to write, but having grown up poor—and a mere girl, at that—my education was quite limited. Still, I tried to inscribe his words upon my heart. I tried to memorize his stories so I might one day be able to tell my grandchildren, hoping that perhaps they, unlike their parents, would have ears to hear.

14

The darkness surrounds me as I pull my blanket more tightly around my shoulders. I long for this night to end. I remember his words—*"I am the light of the world. Whoever believes in me will no longer live in darkness but will have the light of life!"*

Now I understand that Jesus was speaking of spiritual enlightenment and not physical darkness, but as I sit here in the black of night, I cannot help but feel that our light has been extinguished. *Where are you, my Lord? Will you ever return with your light?*

I remember another time when I thought Jesus was removing himself and his light from us. It was during this past year, the last year of his life, that Jesus began to pull away from the crowds and the public speaking. It worried me at first. I could not understand why he would do such a thing—especially after he had gained such widespread popularity and influence. But John told me that Jesus's intent was to focus more of his time and energy to teach his disciples with more intensity than he had been able to teach the large groups. And, as much as I missed sitting among the crowds and listening to his words of life, I had to respect his decision. He was, after all, God's Son. I trusted that he knew what he was doing.

So it was time for me to return to Nazareth again. Now, certainly, my children were pleased to have me home during this period—well, at least initially. And, to my surprise, I felt a new sense of fulfillment being back with them. It actually seemed that I was putting something important into practice—something I had heard from one of Jesus's followers.

My friend Mary of Magdala told me, as we were parting ways, "The Lord said that if we seek to gain our own lives, we will lose them . . . but if we give up our lives for his sake, we will gain them."

Somehow I knew after hearing those words that it was time for me to go home. It seemed that every time I returned to Nazareth after hearing Jesus's preaching, there was an enormous letdown. It always felt a bit like dying to me. As if I truly was losing my life.

But I hoped that this time might be different, and I was more determined than ever to share the truth and the stories I had heard during this past year. Although, I quickly figured out—no great surprise here—that my own children were not the least bit interested in listening to me. Nor were most of my neighbors. However, I soon discovered that they did not appear to mind if I told their children my "childish stories," as everyone began to call them. I suspect the young mothers in our town may have simply enjoyed knowing that their children were occupied and out of harm's way for a spell each day.

So it became something of a ritual, in the late afternoon while mothers were busy with food preparations, that my grandchildren and their friends gathered around me in the shade of my garden as I repeated their uncle's parables. These little ones would listen with wide eyes, and, to my amazement, they never questioned the truth of these stories. Sometimes I think they understood the stories even better than I did. Now, those were wonderful times.

"Tell the one about the shepherd," urged Thomas, my oldest grandson. He was almost eight at the time.

So I launched into the story of the good shepherd and his hundred sheep and how distressed he was when one lamb became lost.

"Where are you?" I said, holding my hand above my forehead and peering out into the distance. I was pretending to be the shepherd. "Where is my little lost lamb?"

The children made baaing noises, and we laughed.

"It is dark on the mountain," I said. "And my little lamb is in danger of getting eaten by a wolf or a bear." Then Thomas stood up and growled, and the children squealed with delight. And on we went until we finally rescued the little lost lamb and he was returned to the flock, where a great celebration took place. Then the children cheered, and sometimes I gave them barley cakes or dried dates as a treat for our own festivities.

As word spread among the children, our little story time in the garden began to get larger. Of course, all were welcome there. To my surprise, instead of feeling bad that I was stuck in my hometown instead of hearing the Lord's teachings, which I did sorely miss, I found great comfort in repeating his stories to the children. Perhaps this was my own way of losing my life for his sake. Who can know such things?

I knew that word of my storytelling was spreading among the adult community in Nazareth, and it became obvious that some thought me quite strange and eccentric for spending so much time with children. Some even believed I was becoming a fanatic. But it was not long before something unexpected started to happen.

I adopted the habit of going to the well quite early in the morning. Of course, I knew that my daughters-in-law and daughters were willing to bring my water for me. But often they did not go until the sun was high, and I have always been concerned about watering my plants in the heat of the day. Besides, I enjoyed walking through our sleepy village, and it was reassuring to know that the larger crowds of women (including the ones who liked to whisper about "that crazy mother of Jesus," as they often called me) would not be there yet. And then there was the quiet cool of the morning to greet me. So this was not an unpleasant task for me.

As time passed, I began to notice that two of my neighbor women started coming to the well while I was there. These were women I had known most of my life. They were only a few years younger than me, but, like me, they had reached an age where child rearing and household responsibilities were not as demanding as they had once been. And it was not long before these two women began talking to me. At first it seemed to be friendly small talk. But I soon realized by their questions and comments that they were genuinely interested in hearing about my son.

I invited these women to meet me in my garden on certain mornings, and there, in the privacy of herbs and vegetables, I told them all I could about Jesus's teachings and his ministry.

"I have heard that he heals the blind," said Rachel, the more talkative one. "Have you ever seen this for yourself?"

I nodded. "And I have seen him heal cripples too. I once saw a man with legs so twisted he could not even sit up straight. Jesus reached down and touched him, and the man instantly leapt to his feet."

"Incredible!" Myra said.

"My sister who lives in Sepphoris knows a woman a little older than us who had been bleeding for years and years," Rachel said. "Nothing would stop it, and she was very weak and sick. But she had heard about Jesus, and somehow she pushed her way through a crowd, and

173

when she barely touched your son's outer garment, she was instantly healed."

"So many miracles . . ." I sighed. "How can it be that everyone does not believe in him?"

Although it was only two rather insignificant women and many small children whom I was able to share these truths with, I was so very thankful for those times. In some ways, they became like my family, making my time at home happier than it had been since Jesus had first left for his ministry.

When the harvesttime came, my children invited me to travel with them to Jerusalem for the Feast of Tabernacles. Now, unlike Passover, this is not a journey we make every year, but it had not slipped my attention that all my children had seemed more religious and devout lately. I did not feel it was so much their eldest brother's influence on them, perhaps, as it was a competition of sorts. My sons were reading more and more at the temple, even choosing sections from the old prophets. I had to wonder if they thought they might be able to perform their way into their eldest brother's acceptance, or perhaps even mine. I could have been wrong, but it felt like they were up to something.

But when Hannah told me they wanted to invite Jesus to go along with us, I felt certain my children had cooked up some sort of questionable scheme. I tried my best to dissuade them, but it was clear that all my children had already agreed on this plan. They knew Jesus was up near the Sea of Galilee at the time, and James was appointed to go and invite him.

"He refuses to come," James said upon his return the following day.

"Yes, that is like him," Joses said.

"He is too good for us," Hannah added.

I was forced to depart their company for the quiet solitude of my garden. As I sat on my favorite thinking stone, which was also a praying stone, I had to wonder when my children would ever figure this thing out. Were they always to perceive their brother Jesus as only that—their brother? Would they never see who he really was and accept him as the Son of God?

Just the same, we traveled to Jerusalem for the Feast of Tabernacles. I guess I hoped I might see Jesus while we were there, although my children were all certain he would not show. In fact, I think they received some kind of satisfaction from their false conclusion. Perhaps it made them feel they were somehow spiritually superior to their brother. I have no idea. But not long after we had arrived, I heard Jesus was indeed in the city. It was Mary of Magdala who told me the good news.

I ran into her in the marketplace, where we hugged and greeted one another joyfully. I felt as if I was seeing my long-lost relative.

"Have you seen the Lord?" I asked.

She smiled. "He is here, Mary. He decided quite suddenly to come. We have all come up with him."

I inquired after everyone's health, and she assured me that all was well. "And your son is well too."

"It has been so quiet," I told her as I inspected a cabbage. "I have missed his public teaching."

"So have many. But perhaps it is only

for a season." Then her face grew cloudy. "I know I should not be worried," she said. "But I have heard rumors . . ."

"Rumors?"

"The Sanhedrin are plotting against him. They call him a blasphemer and say he breaks the Sabbath."

I nodded. This was not unexpected. Everyone knew that the Sanhedrin, the ruling Jewish council, wielded great power in our country. Even the Romans, who supposedly ruled all the land, allowed the Sanhedrin to police their own people. Other than giving the death penalty, there was little the Sanhedrin could not do. And, according to widespread rumor, most of these men were fiercely opposed to Jesus.

She sighed. "Of course, it is useless for any of us to warn him."

I attempted to smile. "Our Lord will do as he sees fit."

"Yes. I know."

And so we parted ways. I did not ask her to send a greeting to my son. I knew that was not necessary. I only hoped that before we returned to Nazareth I might simply see him. If only for a glance.

Jehovah must have been listening to my heart, for the very next day I was blessed to spot my son in the temple. Although, I must admit that my throat tightened with fear when I realized what was transpiring, for it seemed clear that the Sanhedrin were up to something. They were there in great number, almost as if to corner my son. Then suddenly one of the Pharisees thrust a young woman in front of him.

One look at this woman and I had no doubt what she had been caught doing. She was young and beautiful, but her hair and clothing were disheveled, as if she had just been pulled from bed. I had to wonder whose bed it had been. And where was the man who must have been equally involved in this crime? Naturally, that was not mentioned. But mostly it was her expression—eyes cast downward and a tightness to her mouth—that made her offense indisputable.

"Teacher," said the scribe who had assisted the Pharisee in dragging the woman through the temple. "This woman was discovered in the act of adultery."

The Pharisee who still held tightly to the poor woman's arm shoved her to the ground right in front of Jesus. "The law of Moses commands us to stone this woman," the Pharisee said with a face that was red from exertion. "What do *you* say?"

I think I stopped breathing as I watched my son's face, waiting for him to speak. But he said nothing. He simply knelt down, focusing his attention on the ground at his feet as he traced his fingers through the dust. It was almost as if he could not hear the enraged men as they continued yelling and pestering him about this woman and her crime and what was to be done. I think they actually believed they had entrapped him.

"According to our laws, she should be stoned!" the red-faced Pharisee yelled.

Still Jesus continued to scribble in the dust.

I am sure my heart must have stopped beating by then, and I am surprised I did not collapse completely. Finally Jesus stood, and the Sanhedrin and everyone in the temple grew quiet.

"Let him who is without sin among you," he said in a calm but clearly audible voice, "let him be the first one to cast a stone."

Slowly they all began to leave. In fact, everyone, even the bystanders, began to leave. Including me. I heard that not one man was left in that area.

John told me much later that Jesus had then asked the woman about her accusers, and if any of them had condemned her. And when she said no, he told her that he did not condemn her either and that she should go and sin no more.

Of all the things my son has done, this one has probably touched me the most deeply. Why is that? I cannot help but recall a time, thirty-three years ago, when that woman being shamed could have so easily been me. Now, I was not guilty of adultery or fornication, but to be found pregnant outside of marriage would have made it seem like I was. After seeing that woman humiliated like that, so close to being executed, I finally understood why my mother had been so upset back then.

Even though I told her I had been chosen by God, all she could see was that her daughter, if truly pregnant, would be subject not only to the condemnation of the elders but possibly to a stoning as well.

Of course, I have no idea whether Jesus was even mindful of such things on that day when he so graciously excused this woman, who had actually sinned, but I love that he showed such depth of compassion. And I was also quite impressed, perhaps even a bit proud, at how he stumped the members of the Sanhedrin.

Yet this memory brings me frustration tonight. For I cannot understand how it went like that with the Sanhedrin that day and then went so differently just two days ago. Of course, I know Jehovah's ways are much, much higher than mine and no one can second-guess the Almighty. But still I wonder. I am weary with wonder.

15

I must have dozed off, for when I awaken it is with the memory of another dream still stirring freshly within me. Unlike the last one, this dream is not a nightmare; this dream almost gives me hope. In my dream I saw my son Jesus greeting his friend Lazarus. Both were dressed in shining white clothing and smiling. I have no idea what this means, but it does remind me of something that happened not too long ago.

As usual, I went early to the well in Nazareth. As I was walking toward it, I could see Rachel and Myra, and I could tell they were anxious to see me.

"We are so glad you are here," Myra called. "Come, Mary! Come and hear what Rachel has to say."

"I heard the most astounding thing!" Rachel said.

I set down my jug and waited.

"My niece and her husband from Cadasa spent the evening in my house last night. They were on their way home from Jerusalem, where they had been to redeem their firstborn son, Samuel."

"*Come on,* Rachel," Myra urged.

"All right. All right. My cousin said that all around Jerusalem there was talk of a man named Lazarus who lived nearby in Bethany. It seems he had been very sick and then he died."

I nodded, waiting for her to continue, curious as to why this story should concern me.

"This man and his sisters, Mary and Martha—"

"Mary and Martha of Bethany?" I said.

"Yes, I believe they were all from Bethany."

"I think I may know those women," I told her. "Please go on."

"This man, their brother Lazarus, had been dead and in the tomb for *four* days. But Jesus—your son—had men open up the tomb, and then he spoke some words. Oh dear, I wanted to remember them just right for you."

"Do not worry," I assured her. "Just tell me the story."

"I remember!" Rachel's eyes sparkled with excitement. "Jesus told this other Mary that he was the life and, let me think . . . yes, and that he was the resurrection and that if anyone believed in him, even if that person was dead, that person would not stay dead. And that if anyone who was still alive believed in him, that person would never die."

"How can that be?" Myra said. "To never die?"

I just shook my head, unsure of the meaning myself. "Is that all of the story, Rachel?"

"No, no. There is much more! The men opened the tomb where this man Lazarus had been laid out for four days. And then Jesus called out to the dead man, telling him to come out!"

I just stared at Rachel. "And what?" I demanded. "What happened?"

"The dead man came to life, and Jesus told his friends to remove the grave cloths."

I sank to the stone bench that is next to the well. "Oh my."

Myra and Rachel sat down on either side of me. "Is it not amazing?" Myra said.

I nodded.

"Do you think it is true, Mary?" Rachel asked.

I studied her, wondering if her sources, these cousins of hers, were reliable. "You are the one who told us this story. What do you think?"

"Oh yes. I do believe it is true that the man Lazarus rose from the dead. But those other words, the ones Jesus said, that if we believe in him we will not die. Do you think that can possibly be true?"

I took in a deep breath and considered this for a long moment and finally said, "I think if that is what the Son of God said, then it must be true. But I will admit that it sounds fantastic to my ears."

And I must admit that it still sounds fantastic to my ears. Of course, I know now that Jesus did indeed resurrect Lazarus from the dead. I have even met the man, and Lazarus's own sister Mary told me the whole story herself, and in much more detail than Rachel. But it is the middle of this night now, and all I know is this darkness and this silence and that most of the world is asleep, and I know that my son still lies in his tomb, and when morning comes, it will have been three days.

Suddenly I wonder if those words he spoke might possibly be true. First of all, if Jesus truly is the resurrection and the life, then how can he remain dead? And if he is not dead, then why has he not revealed himself to his dearest friends? I do not mean myself, of course. I am only his earthly mother and no one special. But what about John and Simon Peter and Andrew and James and all the others? What about the women like the other Marys, Susanna, Joanna, and the rest who have served him so faithfully? Why would Jesus allow them all to suffer like this if he was truly alive? It makes no sense.

How I long for sleep now. To escape these questions that are hammering inside of my head. *Dear Lord, please help me make it through this night.*

Somehow, blessedly, I find sleep—a quiet and dreamless sleep. And when I awaken I know it is almost morning. The sky is still dark as slate, but I sense that morning is coming. I feel it in my aching bones. The house is still, and no one else is stirring as I slip quietly outside to the terrace to await the morning. I am still weary, and I still feel that I am a hundred years old as I sit on a weathered wooden bench and wait. *Wait for what?* I wonder. Perhaps I am only waiting for the dawn. And when the first light comes, I must decide what I will do next. I think it is time to return to my family, and then, like a dog who has been whipped, I will slink like a shadow back to Nazareth with them. I only hope they do not ask me too many questions. For I fear that I have no answers for them.

How I miss him! My broken heart aches with missing him. And, yes, I must be honest and say that I do miss him as my son, but I miss him as my Lord and Savior even more. How I long to see him again. Not suffering and in pain this time, but smiling and happy. The way I saw him only a week ago.

It was the Sunday before Passover, and Jerusalem was bursting with travelers. We had only just arrived ourselves when we heard that the king would soon be entering the city gates.

"What king is this?" I asked a woman who was holding a palm frond in her hand. "Who is it that you are expecting?"

"The king of Israel!" she shouted with joy.

"Do you mean Jesus?" I asked her.

"Of course!" she exclaimed. "Who else could it be?"

"You are not going to stay for this little show, are you, Mother?" James's voice bore an unmistakable note of disdain.

I nodded. "I most certainly am."

And so my children went on their way, leaving me to stand with the festive crowd that awaited their king's entry into Jerusalem. I stood and waved a palm frond as I saw the small processional passing through. I smiled to myself to note that my son was humbly seated on a young white donkey, just as the prophets of old had predicted. People threw down their outer garments and palm branches to carpet the road as he slowly made his way up to the city gates. Everyone was shouting, saying things like "Hosanna!" or "Blessed is he who comes in the name of the Lord!" It reminded me of the stories I had heard of King David. Only this was Jesus entering Jerusalem!

When Jesus was close enough that I could actually glimpse his face, I could see that he was smiling as he waved at the people. But I also saw great sadness in his eyes. I am not sure anyone else could make it out, but I like to think that, as his mother, I saw it there. To me, it was unmistakable. And despite the joyful greetings and the great sense of expectation in the air, it was as if a dark cloud passed over my soul in that moment, as if I knew this was the beginning of the end.

It makes my head spin to think how quickly those same people turned against my son. Within the week, those same people who had cheered him on as king of Israel were suddenly shouting for him to be crucified. It was unbelievable. Like a horrible dream.

My eyes search out into the east, longing for the sun to make its appearance and drive away this darkness. I can see people beginning to stir now. A pair of women are heading down the street below, probably going to the well. I hear the crowing of a sleepy rooster, and I know it will not be long until daybreak. I long for the sun to come out and warm my weary old bones. But not as much as I long for my Lord. I ache with longing for him.

I pull my cloak more tightly around my shoulders as I remember the last time I saw him smile. I am talking about a real smile, where even his eyes were lit with happiness. The kind of smile he often had as a young child when he had made some new discovery, like catching a frog in midair as it hopped, or seeing the shape of a horse in the clouds, or spotting the first bright green sprout of a bean plant poking its head through the dark spring soil.

Ironically, the last time I saw him smile was on the day of his arrest. Of course, at the time I had no idea he was about to be arrested or to go through such unimaginable torture. To me, it was simply a happy and sunny day. We were well into Passover celebrations by then, and it was the first day of the Feast of Unleavened Bread. I had just been to the market for fresh herbs and was heading back to where my family was staying.

I could hear a boisterous crowd of people moving through the streets behind me, and I naturally thought they might be following Jesus. So I slowed my pace, waiting for them to catch up with me before I turned around to see.

It was always easy to pick my son out of a group, for he is nearly a head taller than most men—and, of course, his face is familiar to me. Surrounded by his disciples, as well as other devoted followers, he paused when he noticed me, and, to my surprise, he looked directly at me.

Thrilled to see him, I smiled and waved, but I continued to walk. I did not want to interrupt Jesus and his disciples on their way, for I suspected they had important matters to attend to. Then suddenly I felt a gentle tap on my shoulder and turned around to see my own son smiling down on me. Oh, what a smile! I stood there for a moment just basking in its warmth. Then he leaned down and whispered in my ear.

"It was your pure heart," he said.

I looked at him curiously.

"The reason my heavenly Father chose you." Then he stooped to pick up something off of the street—how he even noticed it down there was beyond me. But he held it up for me to see. A tiny seed. He smiled again, then placed it in my open palm. "Take good care of it, Mother." And then he continued on his way.

With happy tears in my eyes, I attempted to examine the tiny seed but was unable to identify it. But that is not so unusual. Foreign seeds are often transported when so many travelers from faraway places pass through Jerusalem. Seeds can ride into town stuck in a camel's coat, coming from as far off as Egypt or even Greece. Wherever this mystery seed had come from, I treasured it as I wrapped it in a scrap of soft linen and then tucked it into the pocket I still have sewn into my tunic for just such a purpose.

With all that has happened these last few days, I had nearly forgotten that seed, although I will never forget my son's smile or his words when he gave it to me. Now, worried that I may have lost it, I slip my hand into my secret pocket to see if it is still there. I am relieved to feel its tiny bulge through the fine linen that still surrounds it.

Suddenly, just as the sky grows lighter with the promise of an imminent sunrise, I remember something about seeds. Something I know to be a fact. And the power of its truth almost takes my breath away.

Unless a seed dies, it cannot yield fruit. To bring forth life, there must first be death—or rather, what *appears* to be death. For, you see, only part of the seed dies—only its hard exterior shell. It is the container of the secret of life that actually dies. It may seem like the seed is dead as it sleeps in darkness, and if you dug it up and examined it closely, you would most certainly believe it was dead. But it is very much alive. For only the outer part of the seed dies—and that is so the rest of it can live. In due time the miraculous living part comes forth—in essence, life emerges from death!

As surely as I know this as a gardener, I know now, within the depths of my spirit, that God's Son must rise up again. I know that they have only killed the exterior shell, that which housed God's spirit, the same spirit that remains very much alive in him. I know that in due time, like a seedling, Jesus will burst forth and his life will continue forever—because he is God's Son.

But can I explain this to anyone? I am not sure. Maybe this revelation is just for me. Even so, I thank God the Father and I praise him, for I know that he knows what he is up to. And I will trust that in due time my son—rather God's Son—will be alive and lifted up and exalted!

At long last the sun is up. As I stand and stretch my weary limbs, soaking in the welcome warmth and light, I think this morning is just the sort of morning when life should spring forth out of death. I feel unexplainably at peace.

16

When I go back into the house, others are awake and some of the men are discussing their plans. Unwilling to interrupt them, I wait in the shadows of the doorway.

"It is the third day." John's voice has the distinct ring of hope in it.

"What difference does that make?" Thomas stands at the west window, arms crossed over his chest as he looks outside with a dismal expression. "Jesus is dead."

"But Jesus told us about this. Do you not remember? He said he would die and then rise after three days," John tells him.

"It is over," Thomas says, turning to

face John. "Cannot you see that? Everyone is going home now. You should go home too."

"You are wrong, Thomas," Simon Peter says, suddenly rising to his feet. "I agree with John. Jesus did say he would rise in three days, and we have no reason to doubt him." Then Peter notices me in the doorway. "You are his mother, what do you think?"

"I have no reason to doubt him."

John comes to me. "Mother," he says, reaching to take my hands in his. It warms me to hear how he has taken my son's words to his heart. "Where have you been this morning?"

"On the rooftop," I tell him. "Waiting for the sun to rise."

"So, tell me, do you really believe it is possible?"

I nod and smile. "Where are the women?"

"The two Marys have already gone to the tomb," he says. "They left before the sun came up. They're taking the spices to anoint the body."

I realize now that they must have been

the women I saw down in the street earlier. A part of me wishes I had recognized them and gone out to join them. But another part of me realizes I do not need to go now. For I know in my heart that the Son of God has already risen. I feel it deep within me—the way a mother can sense these things. Noticing that the water jug for the house is nearly empty, I pick it up and begin to go outside but am stopped by John.

"Someone else can do that, Mother," he says.

"I want to do it."

"But Peter and I are going to the tomb now," John tells me. "Do you want to come along?"

"No," I say. "I will wait here."

My heart is at peace as I go down to the well for water. I feel it is my turn to serve, and I am pleased to do so. When I return, the house is quiet and no one seems to be around. So I busy myself with food preparations. I am not sure about the men, but I suspect that the two Marys took no time to eat before they left. As I put together some flat bread and fruit and yogurt for a simple morning meal, I think how generous and kind it is for the women to want to care for Jesus's body first thing today. I felt so bad when we left him there so hastily, due to the coming Sabbath. I fretted over how ill prepared he was for burial. We, especially the women, felt that our Lord deserved much better than that.

But now I am hoping that the women's fragrant oils and preserving spices will be unnecessary. I am hoping that the Son of God will smell like the sweet breath of heaven today. My heart flutters with anticipation as I slice the bread, and I nervously glance out the window to see that it is now midmorning. Still no one has returned.

How I wonder what they will find at the tomb. Or maybe it is too soon for the Son of God to rise. Perhaps I should have gone with them too. But, no, I reassure myself. Let them make this discovery on their own, for they are his closest friends. I am only his mother. Besides, this mother's heart is convinced. I know he lives.

Even so, I am unsure what will happen next. Will Jesus set up an earthly empire here in Jerusalem? That seems unlikely, since he has always said his kingdom is in heaven with the Father. So what then? What comes next?

I manage to eat a small piece of bread along with a few bites of yogurt. Now I am pacing, wondering what is happening at the tomb, and suddenly I am tempted to go up there myself. But I hear voices—women's voices—and they are laughing and calling out my name.

"Mary! Mary!" I hear them call. Now they are in the room, and just one look at their faces and I know! I know without a shadow of doubt.

"He is alive!" I say.

"Yes!" Mary of Magdala claps her hands with joy. "He lives!"

"He is risen!" cries Mary, the mother of James and Salome.

Then we hug each other and dance and shout out praises to Jehovah until we all have tears of joy streaming down our faces.

"Sit and eat," I finally insist, feeling slightly breathless and almost dizzy. "Tell me everything—from start to finish!"

"At first I was so frightened," Mary of Magdala says as she sits at the place I have set for her. "As we were walking we felt the earth tremble and shake. We were still a ways from the tomb, and it reminded me of the day at the cross when the earth quaked and groaned. Worried that something was wrong, I ran on ahead to see what was happening. But when I reached the tomb, I could see that the stone had been rolled away, and the soldiers were nowhere in sight. And the tomb was empty!"

"I was hurrying as fast as I could to join her," the other Mary adds. "But my old legs are not as spry as hers."

"I immediately thought someone had stolen his body," Mary says as she breaks a piece of bread. "I could not understand how the tomb could be empty. The cloth we had wrapped him in was still there, but his body was gone. That is when I began to cry. But then I saw a man. At first I thought he was only a gardener, but then I noticed his brilliant white clothing. 'Where have they taken my Lord?' I asked him."

Mary pauses to catch her breath and to take a bite of bread.

"Tell her," the other Mary says. "Tell her what this man said."

Mary chews and swallows, then continues. "He said, 'Why do you seek the living among the dead?' "

I clap my hands with joy at this. "Who was this man?" I ask her. "Who said this to you?"

"I was not sure. But I knew he was holy, I thought maybe an angel or maybe even our Lord, but all I could do was fall down on my knees . . . I was afraid to look into his face."

"That is when I arrived," the other Mary says. "And when I saw this man in glorious shining garments, I fell to my knees as well."

"Then he spoke again," Mary says. " 'He is not here,' he told us, 'He has risen!' "

"Imagine," the other Mary says, "our joy at hearing that!"

"Then he continued. He said, 'Do you not remember what he told you—how the Son of Man must be delivered into the hands of sinful men, and be crucified, and on the third day rise again?' "

"And that is when we remembered those words," the other Mary says. "That is when it all became clear. Then he told us to come back and tell the others the good news."

"Even so," Mary says. "It was so hard to believe. And suddenly the man was gone and we were all alone in the tomb." She glanced at the other Mary and frowned slightly. "And that is when Mary began to wonder if we had imagined the whole thing."

"I am sorry," the other Mary says. "But it was so astounding. And I was so stunned, I began to worry that it was not real."

"Even so, we headed back here," Mary says. "We were eager to tell the others— to see what they would say. And then we met John and Peter on the road, and I began babbling to them, carrying on like a madwoman, I am sure." Mary's eyes are wide as she uses her hands as a dramatic expression. "I was talking too fast, trying to say too much, and I am afraid they thought my demons had come back and taken control of me again." She throws back her head and laughs. "But we finally made them understand. We both assured them that the tomb was truly empty and that the man there told us Jesus had risen."

"You should have seen those two take off," the other Mary says. "They went running toward the tomb like someone had lit their tails on fire."

"And then we came back here to tell the others." Mary looks around as if she has only just noticed the empty room. "Where is everyone?"

"I think they have given up," I admit sadly. "Most of them are probably heading for home now."

"Oh, why could they not wait?" she cries. "Why did not they have faith?"

It is not long before John and Peter return. Both of them are nearly hysterical with joy. "He is alive!" John cries when he sees me. "Jesus has risen from the dead, just as he said—three days and he is risen!" He grabs my hands and dances around the room with me.

"We saw him for ourselves," Peter says

with more hope than he has shown in days. "He met us on the road. At first we did not even recognize him. But then he spoke, and we knew it was our Lord."

"He told us to come back here and tell the brethren," John says with excitement. "He told us to meet him in Galilee."

"Where is everyone?" Peter asks, noticing that the rooms are empty.

"I think they've gone home," I tell the men. "I went out to get water, and when I returned no one was here."

Thomas walks into the house. His face is still sullen and sad.

"Thomas! Thomas!" John shouts. "He is alive! Our Lord has risen!"

But Thomas looks unconvinced. "How do you know this?"

"We saw him with our own eyes," Peter says.

"We saw him too," Mary of Magdala says.

"That is impossible," Thomas says. "I will not believe it until I see him for myself."

"But it is true," John says. "He is—"

"I will not believe it," Thomas says stubbornly. "Not until I see him myself and actually put my fingers through the nail holes of his hands."

"Then come with us, dear doubting friend," John says in a cheerful voice. "Come with us to Galilee. And there you can see him for yourself."

A couple of the other men trickle in, and they too are astonished at the news, but very quickly the men are packed and ready to travel. And the women are cleaning things up and making plans to follow soon after.

"What about you, Mary?" John asks before they leave. "Are you coming too?"

I shake my head. "Not yet," I tell him. "But I will join you later."

He smiles. "Good. Remember that your son, my Lord, has charged me—you are my mother and I am your son. I cannot lose you now."

"Do not worry," I assure him. "You will not lose me."

After the men leave, I help the women pack up the things in the house. They continue to urge me to come with them, but I sense in my spirit that it is not time for me to leave just yet. I sense there is something I must do here before I travel to Galilee.

"Then meet us there," Mary urges as they pause at the door. "Come and stay with me in my home in Magdala by the Sea of Galilee. You know I will welcome you with open arms."

So I bid them good-bye and promise to join them in Magdala as soon as I can.

When everyone is gone, I feel strangely lonely. It is as if my family has left me. And it is true, they have become like family to me. Even so, I know there is a chore I must do. I pray as I pack my things. I pray that Jehovah will help me.

I peer this way and that as I go down the streets of Jerusalem. I know I am hoping that I will see him too—that my risen Lord will suddenly appear before me and I will know, with no shadow of doubt, that he is alive. But soon I arrive where my family and my sister Sarah's family have been staying this past week. I can see that they too are getting ready to go home now. But in a loud voice that is rather unlike me, I call out to them, saying I have an important announcement to make. I can see they are surprised to see that I have returned, but I know I have my relatives' attention as they stop what they are doing and gather around to listen to me. Feeling nervous and uncertain, I pray that my Lord will help give me the right words.

"There is news," I begin. "You know by now that my son Jesus was brutally killed just three days ago. He was viciously beaten and then nailed to the cross." I pause and notice how quiet it gets as their eyes look downward and they solemnly nod. And I see that my Hannah has tears streaming down her cheeks, and even my usually resolute James looks quite distraught. For the first time I think maybe they actually do care about their brother, at least a bit more than they have shown. "And, as you may know, after he died, just before Sabbath, Jesus was laid in a tomb that was donated by a kind stranger."

"Joseph of Arimathea," adds my sister Sarah, who was with me that day. "One of the few good men of the Sanhedrin."

"That is right," I say. "And soldiers were placed as guards at the tomb, and the doorway was sealed with a large stone." I pause, and I can see they are growing quite curious as they wait for me to continue. "A miracle has happened today," I tell them. "Jesus has risen from the dead. The grave could not hold him. Like a seed that is planted into the ground and must die before it comes to life, Jesus, although he was dead, is now very much alive."

I can tell by their faces that they are completely shocked. But there is a mixture of reactions in the group. Some appear skeptical, some are confused, and a few of the older children look hopeful. Still no one speaks.

"Is it true?" Sarah finally asks in a barely audible voice. "Is he really alive, Mary? Have you actually seen him?"

"I have not seen him for myself. But Peter and James saw him. And some of the other women saw an angel who told them—"

"Then how can you be sure, Mother?" Joses asks. "What if they are deceiving you?"

"Because I know in here," I tell them in a loud voice, tapping my forefinger upon my chest. "I know in my heart. I know that Jesus is alive just as much as I know that he is the Son of God and as much as I know that he will rule and reign in God's kingdom forever. I know."

No one says anything after that. Sarah pulls me aside. "Have you been to see the tomb yet?"

I shake my head.

"Let us go," she urges me. "Let us go together."

And so as the others begin to discuss what I have just told them (and I can hear an argument beginning because some are filled with rigid unbelief while others are unsure), Sarah and I slip away. Hand in hand, with the late morning sun on our faces, we walk toward the tomb.

"Do you remember," Sarah says as we walk, "when Jesus told everyone not to lay up treasures for themselves here on earth, where moth or rust can destroy or where thieves can break in and steal?"

I nod. "I do remember."

"And that instead we should lay up for ourselves treasures in heaven, for where our treasure is, there our hearts will be also?"

"Yes. Why do you mention that now?"

"Because if what you say is true, if Jesus really is alive, I want to live my life like that. I want to give all I have to serve him."

I smile and squeeze her hand. "So do I." Of course, I know Sarah has much more earthly treasure than I do. Even so, I am happy to give what little I have to do the will of my Lord.

Finally we reach the burial grounds, and it is just as they have said. The stone is rolled away, and the tomb is empty. Sarah and I stand in the empty tomb for a long moment, enveloped in silence and awe. Then we both fall to our knees and quietly worship our King. We both know he has risen.

"What will happen now?" Sarah asks when we finally head back to the city. "Where will Jesus go? Will he rule his people as the king of Israel?"

"I am not sure," I admit. "I only know that he asked his disciples to meet him in Galilee."

"*Where* in Galilee?" she asks with the

same enthusiasm she had as a child. "Can we go there? Can we meet him too?"

I laugh. "I am not sure exactly where. I do not think even the men knew for sure. But Mary has invited me to come and stay at her home in Magdala. Would you like to come too?"

Sarah throws her arms around me, hugging me tightly. "Oh yes!" she cries. "Let us leave at once."

17

When we get back to our families, they are packed and ready to leave. In fact, some have already started out, promising to meet the others just north of the city.

"You are coming with us, Mother?" Hannah asks with surprise.

I smile. "If I am welcome."

She hugs me. "Of course you are welcome. You are our mother."

And so we travel, and I walk with light feet and a happy heart. But no mention is made of Jesus. Not one word is said about either his death or his resurrection as we move slowly northward. During the first day of our journey, other than Sarah and my grandchildren, most of my relatives and neighbors seem to be keeping a safe distance from me, as if they do not quite know what to make of me. Even my Hannah, who seemed so glad I was joining them, stays ahead of me in the group.

"Do you remember the story Jesus once told about the Samaritan?" Sarah says in a voice loud enough that others might hear. Then she nods at me as if I am to continue from there.

"Yes, I do," I say, also in a clear voice that draws my grandchildren's attention. "Jesus said we need to love our neighbors. But then someone asked him, 'Who are my neighbors?' Do you remember that, Sarah?"

"Yes, and that is when Jesus told about the man who was traveling to Jerusalem. Now, what happened to him? Do you recall, Mary?"

I smile at her, knowing full well that she knows what happened. Using my best storytelling voice, I begin. "A man from Jericho was out on the road one night. He was all by himself when suddenly he was attacked by bandits! The poor man was stripped, robbed, and beaten nearly to death by these wicked men. It was horrible!"

I notice that our fellow travelers are walking a little nearer to us now, almost as if they too wish to hear this frightening story. So I continue. "Well, this unfortunate man was lying alongside the road, naked and bleeding, and along came a priest who was also on his way to Jerusalem, but when he saw the poor naked man barely breathing next to the road, he just hurried along his way."

Several people make *tsk-tsk* sounds as if that priest was not a very nice fellow, but they say nothing. "Next there came a Levite, also heading for Jerusalem, but he heard the cries of the injured man. He paused to look down at him, but then he quickly crossed over to the other side of the road and continued on his way."

"That is horrible," I hear a neighbor murmur.

"Finally, just as the beaten man was about to give himself up for dead, a man from Samaria came down the road." I pause long enough to allow them to think about this, and I can tell by their smug faces that they are certain a Samaritan will treat the unfortunate traveler far worse than the others had. The Samaritans are despised by my people. Maybe they even imagine the Samaritan will actually slit the poor man's throat.

"Well, the Samaritan sees the wounded man, and immediately he stops. He gives the man wine and pours oil on his wounds and then bandages him up and gently loads him onto his donkey and takes him to an inn in Jerusalem, and there the Samaritan stays and cares for the ailing man until he is better. Then the Samaritan pays the innkeeper a good amount of money to continue caring for the man until he is well enough to travel."

Now some of my neighbors and relatives are murmuring, questioning whether something like this could ever actually happen. "So, Sarah," I say to my sister. "Which of those men was the neighbor to the man who had been attacked by thieves?"

"Well, if I was that poor man, I would

have to choose the Samaritan as my neighbor," she says.

"I agree. And that is the kind of neighbors we should be too. When Jesus said to love our neighbors, he meant that we should love everyone we meet, no matter who they are or where they are from."

"What if that person you meet is Herod?" my cousin Nathan asks. I can tell by the tone of his voice that he means to taunt me. "What if we are talking about the man who sentenced your son to death? Tell me, do you also love *him*?"

I carefully consider this before I answer, deciding that I can only be honest. "The truth is, Nathan, I do not feel much love for Herod right now. But Jesus commands us to love our enemies and to pray for those who persecute us."

"So do you *love* Herod, Mary?"

"I am *willing* to love Herod, but I may need my Lord's help to do so. Right now I am working just to forgive Herod, and I must admit even that is difficult."

Sarah puts her hand on my shoulder. "It is a start."

I sigh. "It is much easier now than it was

yesterday when Jesus was still in the tomb." Of course, this is where I lose Nathan's attention. His expression tells me he has no interest in hearing of this. And I can tell that any mention of Jesus rising from the dead makes all of my neighbors and relatives very uncomfortable.

However, I am excited to share this news with my good friends Rachel and Myra. I know they are traveling with a group that is ahead of us and that they started out even before daybreak.

I am so pleased to find them when we finally make camp at nightfall.

"Oh, Mary," Rachel exclaims, taking me into her arms before I have a chance to speak. "I have been so distressed for you and your great loss."

Myra stands quietly to one side, but I see tears building in her eyes as I step back from Rachel.

"But I have good news," I begin, and then I pour out the wondrous story of Jesus's resurrection.

"Is it really true?" Rachel asks with

hopeful brows. "Have you seen him for yourself?"

"Not yet," I explain. "But I believe I will." I tell them of my plan to continue on to Galilee, where he has promised to meet the men.

"And then you will return to Nazareth and tell us what has happened?" Rachel says.

"Of course," I reassure my friends.

During our nine-day journey back to Nazareth, Sarah and I continue to repeat things we have heard from Jesus, telling his parables and describing some of the miracles we have witnessed. To our surprise, a few of our relatives and neighbors grow more interested with each passing day. Or maybe we are simply the entertainment for those who are bored and road weary. *But at least they are listening,* I tell myself, and I think perhaps Jesus's death—whether they believe in his resurrection or not—has gotten their attention.

We arrive in Nazareth just before dusk on the ninth day of travel, and I invite Sarah's family to spend the night with us. But in the morning, as they repack for the last leg of their journey back to Cana, I likewise pack my own things.

"Where are you going now, Mother?" James demands when he sees me heading out the door of my house. I suspect my daughter-in-law, Joses's wife, has informed on my activities, but I do not mind.

"On to Galilee," I announce as I continue to go out the door, holding my head up.

He is walking beside me now, his hand on my arm almost as if he means to stop me, which I think is quite ridiculous. "Why, Mother?"

I turn and attempt to smile at him. Oh, how I wish he could understand. "I hope . . ." I begin. "I hope it is to see my Lord."

He stops walking as a frown creases his dark brow. "Do you still believe in that nonsense? That Jesus has risen from the dead?"

I stop in the middle of the street, looking into my second oldest son's eyes for a long moment before I say, "I am your mother, James. Would I lie to you?"

He shakes his head and looks some-what embarrassed.

"If I say he has risen, and everyone who has seen him says he has risen, why cannot you believe he has risen?"

He shrugs, looking down at his sandals the same way he used to do as a small boy who had been caught at mischief.

"Listen to me, James," I speak in an urgent voice now. "This is not a lie, this is not a game, this is very real. Your half brother, Jesus from Nazareth, truly is the Messiah. Whether you like it or not, he *is* the Christ, the Son of the Living God. And if you do not believe me, you should go and talk to Jesus's disciples up in Galilee. You should hear them tell you of all he has done, the miracles, the teaching, the fulfillment of prophecy. Maybe you would believe them."

James takes in a deep breath, then quietly says, "I have been studying the old prophets, Mother, and I can see that some of their words do align with some circumstances in my brother's life."

I am so stunned that I am barely able to form words. "So . . . are you . . . have you been considering this?" I finally manage to ask.

"I remember a day," James looks over my head toward the synagogue, "before all this craziness began . . . or perhaps it was even the beginning. It was on the Sabbath, and Jesus was in the synagogue and, as he often did, he stood to read from the scroll. A priest handed him the book of the prophet Isaiah, and Jesus opened it up and began to read. Do you know what he read?"

I nod and wait.

" 'God's spirit is on me,' Jesus read out loud that day. 'Because he has anointed me to preach good news to the poor. He has sent me to heal the brokenhearted and to deliver the captives, to return sight to the blind, to set the oppressed free, and to declare the year of our Lord.' "

"You know those words by heart?"

"I did after that day."

"But still you do not believe?"

He sadly shakes his head.

"But you are considering these things now?"

His countenance brightens just slightly.

"I am. Go on your way to Galilee, Mother. And if the Son of God is truly there, send word back to me, and I will join you."

I grab my second oldest son and pull him toward me for a long, hard hug. When I release him I have tears in my eyes. Tears of gladness. "I will do as you say," I promise him.

Then I hurry along to join Sarah and her family. But as I leave Nazareth I am filled with great hope and intense joy. I know I should be weary with travel by now, but suddenly I feel I could walk for years and over mountains if it was my Lord's will.

After we reach Cana Sarah and I spend a night in her home, and the next morning we bid her children and grandchildren farewell and turn eastward to continue our journey on toward Galilee.

"So much has happened," Sarah says as we walk at our own comfortable pace—the pace of two grandmothers who enjoy one another's company. "So much is changing, Mary. And so much more will change. I can feel it in my bones."

"Yes," I agree. "And I am so curious about Jesus's twelve disciples. Do you think they all heard the good news and went on to Galilee? Do you suppose they have met up with him yet?"

"Mary," says Sarah in a tentative voice. She quits walking and puts her hand on my arm to stop me. Then she looks at me, but her face is lined in sadness. "Do you not know that there are only eleven disciples now?"

"Eleven?"

"Have you not heard about Judas?"

"Judas?" I ask. "Which Judas?"

"Iscariot." Her voice is quite solemn now.

"What are you saying?"

"Did you not know that he, Judas Iscariot, was the betrayer?"

I consider this. "I heard some talk of a betrayer," I admit. "But it was right after the crucifixion, and I was so heavy with grief that I am sure I did not pay much attention."

"I can understand that," Sarah says. "But during the days following Jesus's death, everyone in Jerusalem talked of little else. They spoke of how it all happened and why and who, and, well, you know how stories can circulate."

"So the betrayer was one of Jesus's own?" I am still trying to take this in. "And it was Judas Iscariot?" I try to remember this young man whom I knew only briefly. He was one of the more learned of Jesus's twelve. By the time I met him, I had assumed that Jesus would only surround himself with people such as fishermen and craftsmen, and I was somewhat surprised that the nicely dressed and well spoken Judas Iscariot became part of the group. Although he was kind and well mannered, he never seemed to quite fit in with the others.

"It makes no sense," Sarah says. "They say Judas turned Jesus over to the temple guards for a miserly thirty pieces of silver. The cost of a mere slave!"

"Why would he do that?"

"Some say Satan entered his heart."

I feel a chill run down my spine.

"Perhaps Jehovah is the only one who knows these things for sure, Mary."

"What became of Judas?"

"They say he came to regret what he

had done and that he returned to the temple and threw the money back at the priests, begging them to undo what had already begun. But it was too late." She sighed. "He later hanged himself."

"Oh!"

"Do you think there will be resurrection and life for Judas?" Sarah asks.

"I think only the Lord can answer that question. But I do remember the thief on the cross next to Jesus, the one who was sorry and contrite."

Sarah nodded. "And Jesus said he would be in paradise that very day."

But I do not know about poor Judas Iscariot. However, I am thankful that I did not learn of this sooner, for I am afraid it would be hard to forgive the man who betrayed my son—a man who had supposedly been a friend. But it is easier to think about this now that I know Jesus is alive. To my surprise, I feel mostly pity for Judas the betrayer.

We rest in the shade during the heat of the day, then start out again as the shadows grow longer. Soon we can tell we are nearing Magdala. The smell of fresh lake air drifting on a gentle breeze cools our faces, and we both quicken our pace.

It is not the first time I understand why Jesus loves it here by the Sea of Galilee. The sun dips low as we enter the town that nestles onto the hillside next to the lake. We stop and ask for directions and then quickly find the right house, which is easy to spot because of its prominence. Then, just as promised, we are warmly welcomed into Mary's comfortable home, and she tells us that we are just in time for the evening meal. But I am much hungrier for information than I am for food.

18

"Please, Mary," I beg after Sarah and I have washed and been seated at the table on the terrace that overlooks the lake. "Please, tell us what has happened. We are starving for news. Has Jesus met with his disciples yet? Have you seen him?"

Joanna, Susanna, and Mary, the mother of James and Salome, are also staying with Mary, as are a few others. We are all sharing this evening meal together, and I cannot help but notice how everyone looks much more relaxed and happy since the last time I saw all these women.

"So much is happening," our hostess

says as servants begin to bring dishes heaped with food. "Where do I begin?"

"We feel certain now that it was actually Jesus who met us at the tomb," the other Mary says. "After we heard accounts of others who have met him. It seems that many do not recognize him at first, for he is changed."

"Changed?" I ask, feeling a shadow of concern.

"Glorified," Mary, our hostess, says. "They say he no longer seems so much like an earthly man."

"Except that he still has holes in his hands," Joanna says.

"Yes," Mary says with wide eyes. "He has even revealed himself to Thomas. They say he told Thomas to put his finger right through the holes in his hands as well as the puncture wound in his side. And Thomas obeyed."

"Oh my!"

"Then the Lord said to Thomas, 'You believe because you have seen me. I will bless the ones who believe in me *without* seeing.' "

I feel a warm rush running through me

as I glance across the table at my sister's smiling face. We both have yet to see him. Perhaps we never will. Nevertheless, we both believe.

"Tell them the fishing story, Mary," Susanna says eagerly. "Indeed, that is a good one."

As we dine on excellent food and wine, enjoying the dusky light on the dark blue lake down below us, Mary begins to speak. "Some of the men were discouraged when they came up here with such enthusiasm but were not met by the Savior. I believe Simon Peter felt worst of all, and he suggested that they return to their old livelihood, which, as you know, is fishing. So they got out their old boats and their nets and set out in the evening to fish. Well, they fished all night, and yet they never caught a single fish." She threw back her head and laughed merrily. "Can you imagine how they felt then? After all they had been through and they could not even remember how to catch fish?"

I shook my head in wonder as I took another bite of tender lamb and waited for her to continue.

"Well, it was morning, and they had just pulled in their empty nets and were ready to give up when they heard a stranger calling to them from the beach. He was telling them to throw their nets out on the *right* side of the boat. Well, you can just imagine how they reacted to that. Here they had been fishing all night without catching a single thing. John said Peter was grumbling something fierce as he reluctantly helped his brother toss the nets out again. But the nets barely touched the water when they began to fill with fish."

I know now that the stranger on the beach *must* have been Jesus, but I listen quietly as Mary continues her story.

"So they dragged their bulging nets to shore and climbed out of their boat to thank this man, and he had already gotten a fire going on the beach, and he invited them to join him for breakfast. Of course, they were curious as to who this man was, although they strongly suspected it was the Lord by then. But when he broke the bread and fed them the fish, they were absolutely certain it was him. It was the third time he had shown himself to them."

"But tell them about Simon Peter," Susanna urges.

"Yes, yes," Mary says. "I almost forgot. Andrew told me about this. It seemed that even though Peter was glad the Lord was alive, he still felt miserable for the way he had denied him on the day of his death. Well, after they had finished their breakfast, Jesus took Peter aside and said to him, 'Simon Peter, do you love me?' And, naturally, Peter said yes. And Jesus said, 'Then feed my lambs.' But then Jesus asked him the exact same question again. And once again, Peter said yes. And Jesus said, 'Tend my sheep.' And then . . ." Mary pauses, I think to catch her breath, but I can hardly wait to hear the rest of this story.

Her eyes grow wide with excitement, and she even stands up as she continues. "Jesus asked Peter this exact same question a third time. And, of course, Peter was just falling apart by then, poor man, and he cried out, 'Lord, you know all things! You know I love you!' And then Jesus simply said once again, 'Feed my sheep.' "

"Three times!" Susanna exclaims. "You

see, Mary? Jesus wanted Peter to have three times to make him feel better."

"Oh, that is absolutely wonderful," I say as I clap my hands. "I am so happy for Simon Peter. He must be so relieved."

"You have never seen anyone so joyful," Mary says as she sits back down at the table and sighs. "Truly, Peter is a new man."

"And where are the men now?" I ask as Joanna passes me a dish of figs covered in honey.

"They have gone off to the hills with the Lord," the other Mary says. "We have not heard from them since they left."

"And has Jesus revealed himself to any of you again?" I ask.

Mary shakes her head. "No, but it is enough just to know he is here."

"Yes," I tell her. "That is how I feel."

We visit after dinner, sharing our various stories and experiences with each other, and once again I am reminded of how these women feel like family to me. And I think of John, Jesus's beloved disciple, and how he is like a son. Even so, I cannot completely dismiss my own children. I am reminded of my son James and that look of longing in his eyes before I left home yesterday and how he made me promise to send word back to him. Something I shall do first thing in the morning.

Sarah and I share a lovely room to sleep in. I suspect it is the best in the house, and I am honored that Mary is so generous. The room has a window that overlooks the lake, and although I should be exhausted from travel, I still feel a lightness and joy in my spirit, and after I hear the quiet breathing of my sleeping sister, I arise from my bed and go to look out the window. The stars are shining brightly, reflected like glistening jewels on the surface of the smooth, dark lake. I think to myself, *He is out there right now.* My son—rather, the Son of God—is out there with his disciples tonight.

Then I return to my bed and sleep more soundly than I have slept in weeks.

When I wake up I hear the sounds of voices in the house. Male voices—and they sound happy. I hurry to dress, and, without waking Sarah, I slip down to see what is happening. I hope to see that Jesus is here. But when I get down to the main room, I see only Peter and John.

"Mother!" John cries when he sees me. He hurries over and hugs me. "It is so good to see you again. Have you heard all the wonderful stories about our Lord?"

I nod, smiling. "I am so happy."

"Jesus has just left," he informs me, but I try not to show the disappointment I feel at this news. "Before he left he gave us some important messages. As soon as everyone is up, I will share his news with all the women."

Before long, we are all gathered around the table again. Mary's servants have prepared a very elegant breakfast for everyone. I must admit that I am beginning to feel like a queen. And while it is an interesting change for me, I am not completely comfortable with this luxurious lifestyle. Still, I am grateful to Mary for her gracious hospitality.

After we finish eating, Simon Peter stands to address the group. I instantly recognize what Mary has been saying about how he has changed. I definitely see something different in his eyes. It is a mixture of confidence and peace, and what I might best describe as humility. Yes, I do believe this fisherman has changed!

"Jesus took us into the hills," he begins slowly, putting emphasis on each word. "And while we were there, Jesus told us that all authority in heaven and earth has been given to him." He pauses, allowing us a moment to absorb these words.

"After that, Jesus charged us to go out and to make disciples of all nations. He said that we are to baptize them in the name of the Father, the Son, and the Holy Spirit. And that we are to teach them all the things he has taught and commanded to us."

The room is completely silent, and I feel that everyone in here believes that this message is for each one of us personally. Then Peter continues. "Finally Jesus said, 'Remember, I am with you always, even to the end of time.' "

I run these words through my mind again. *"Remember, I am with you always, even to the end of time."* I repeat this to myself several times until I am certain that this promise will be etched upon my heart.

"Is that all?" our hostess asks, and I feel sure she speaks for all the women, for that is the exact question on the tip of my tongue.

"No," John says. "There is something else. The Lord has commanded for all of us, for all who believe in him, to meet in Jerusalem and to wait there for him to bring us power from on high."

"And he will meet us there?" I ask hopefully.

"That is what we believe," John says with a cheerful smile.

"We will leave at once," Peter announces. "You are welcome to travel with us if you are ready. Or we can meet up with you later."

Plans are quickly made. Oh, how I appreciate Mary's ability to take charge for the rest of the women. She is so assured, and her mind is sharp and quick to remember what is needed. Finally she decides that we will travel on our own and that she will send a messenger ahead of us to arrange our stay with Mary and

Martha near Jerusalem. There we will tarry until the men have determined where we shall gather to wait for the return of our Lord.

"I am so sorry that you have to travel again so soon," Mary tells me as we set out on our journey the following morning.

I laugh. "Do not be worried," I assure her. "I may be old, but my legs are as sturdy as a donkey and my heart is as light as a dove. I think I could walk forever as long as I knew I would meet up with my Lord in the end."

It is the second day of our trip when we reach Nazareth just before noon. I have already told Mary of Magdala about my son James and his growing interest in his half brother, and we have agreed to take our midday rest in the same town that once made the Son of God feel very unwelcome.

And I cannot say that my neighbors make us feel any more welcome on this day. We receive bold stares, and people hold their hands before their mouths as they whisper to one another. One can only imagine what they are saying. But, determined to ignore this, I take my sister travelers to my humble home, where I am determined to make them welcome. My daughter-in-law, Joses's wife, is surprised to see us coming. And although this is my home, one that I share with my sons and their wives, I sense that I am intruding into her space.

"We have only come to rest for a spell," I quickly assure her. There is no sense in letting her think that my friends and I will be here for longer than that. "After our rest and after the heat of day passes, we will have something to eat, and then we will continue on our way." Now, it is our custom that young women show respect to their elders, particularly daughters-in-law to their husbands' mothers. A normal response to my announcement would be to offer to help and to serve us food. But Joses's wife simply nods, then goes on her own way. Not unlike a slap in the face.

I tell the women to make themselves comfortable in my modest home, then go off in search of James. As expected, I find him in the workshop, but, to my surprise, my Hannah is also there. I tell Hannah I have guests who are hungry and tired, and, since James has no wife, ask if she could attend to them. Maybe I have raised my daughters well—although I do not deserve such credit—because as I take little Mary into my arms, Hannah departs to see to the task of preparing food for my friends.

"What is my mother doing now?" James asks as he sets aside a saw.

I tell him all the news from Galilee, and I can see that this makes an impression on him.

"So you are going to Jerusalem again?" he asks as he removes his work apron and then shakes the sawdust from it.

"We will leave as soon as the heat of day has passed."

He frowns. "I have some things I must attend to first. But when I am done, may I join you down there?"

I smile. "Of course! I would be delighted to see you there." I tell him where we will be staying, with Martha and Mary, and he promises to meet me before the second Sabbath.

"Shall I invite others?" he asks in an uncertain voice.

"Yes!" I urge him. "Invite anyone who will come. All of your brothers and sisters are more than welcome. Any who believe in the Son of God are welcome."

He makes a half smile. "I do not imagine we will have much of a traveling crowd, Mother. Not from *this* town, anyway."

I nod with understanding. After all, this is Nazareth. "Even if it is only you, James, you are most welcome."

19

We are soon on our way, and we seem to be growing in numbers as we go. I am pleasantly surprised, just as we are leaving Nazareth, when I discover that my dear friends Rachel and Myra want to join us. They have hastily packed and are ready to travel.

"The more the merrier," I tell them as we hug. Then I introduce them to my other women friends. "So far, these two are the only other true followers of Jesus in my hometown."

"And that is only because of Mary," Rachel adds.

I laugh, then say, "And that is only because of Jesus."

After a couple of hours, Mary of Magdala announces that we will spend the night in the town of Nain. "We have friends there," she tells us.

"Nain?" I say to Mary as we get closer to the town, which is just south of Nazareth. "Is not that where Jesus raised a boy from the dead?"

"Yes," she says. "I saw it with my own eyes."

"Can you tell us about it?" I ask.

"Yes," Rachel urges. "Please tell us, Mary."

Mary smiles, and I think, not for the first time, that this woman is a born storyteller. "We had recently been in Capernaum," she begins. "Do you remember hearing of the centurion who asked Jesus to heal his servant?"

"Yes," I answer. "I heard that the centurion's faith was so strong that he told Jesus it was unnecessary for him to come to his home, that he knew if the Lord said, 'Be healed,' the servant would be healed."

"That is right," Mary says. "And even

Jesus marveled at the man's faith. Well, we had come down from Capernaum and decided to visit Nain, just as we are doing today, but when we reached the gate, we could see that a funeral procession was just coming through. Quite a large one, in fact, for the woman who had lost her son was well respected in the city. As soon as we saw this woman's face, we could see that she was distraught and broken-hearted. She was so overcome with grief that a couple of her friends were helping her walk. It turned out that not only had she lost her son, but her husband had recently died as well, and now she was all alone."

"Poor woman," I murmur.

"Yes," Mary says. "You, of all women, should understand." She puts her hand on my shoulder as we walk. "Now, Jesus felt very sorry for this woman, and he stopped and kindly said, 'Do not weep.' Then he went over to where some men were carrying the open casket, and he put his hand upon it and said, 'Young man, arise.' "

Our traveling group grows very quiet. It

is clear that we are all waiting for her to finish the story.

"And the boy sat up, right there in the casket, and he actually began to speak. It was marvelous! Then Jesus said, 'Here, woman, I give you your son.' "

"Can you imagine?" my sister exclaims. "What joy that woman must have felt!"

"That is for certain," Mary says. "And the whole city was amazed. Many of the people in the funeral procession fell onto their knees, and, praising Jehovah, they proclaimed Jesus to be a great prophet. And, indeed, he received a prophet's welcome in their town."

Not like it was in his hometown, I think sadly.

"And so," she finishes, "we have friends here in Nain."

As it turns out, Mary is right. We do have friends here in Nain. Word of our arrival reaches the city boundaries even before we get there. Just as we enter the city gates, we are greeted by a woman and a young man. "Welcome, welcome!" the woman is calling as she hurries toward us. "I have heard that friends of the Lord were blessing our town with their company," she says to Mary of Magdala. "I hope that you will grace me with your presence in my humble home."

Mary smiles and nods. "We would be honored."

So it is that we follow this woman and her son to a large home in the center of the city. As soon as we arrive we are treated with great respect.

"This is Mary from Nazareth," Mary says as she introduces us to our hostess. "She is the mother of our Lord."

The woman turns her full attention to me now, and, taking both my hands into her own, her eyes fill with tears. "Oh, my dear friend," she says through her sobs. "I was so sorry to hear of his death. It is so—"

"No," I tell her. "It is all right now. Have you not heard that the Son of God has risen from the dead?"

Her eyes grow big and then she smiles. "Of course! Of course! Just as he raised my own son from the dead. Of course! It would only make sense that he should rise too!" Then she hugs me tightly and whispers in my ear. "You are to be praised among women."

When she releases me, I smile and say, "I am only a disciple of my Lord. Your sister in Christ."

She nods. "Yes, I understand. But you will take the seat of honor next to me at dinner tonight."

And while such attention is still an embarrassment to me, a poor peasant woman, I can see that this is important to her, so I do not object.

After a fine feast, we all enjoy a good night's rest, and when it is time to leave in the morning, this woman not only gives us more provisions, she asks if she might accompany us to Jerusalem.

"We would love to have you," Mary says.

"Yes!" I agree. "And your son too, if he wants to come."

Well, not only do the mother and son join us, but quite a few people from Nain are coming as well. At this rate, there will be two hundred of us by the time we reach Jerusalem!

On our fourth day of travel, we stop in

Samaria, in a town called Sychar. It is nearly dusk as we pause at the well to refill our skins. As usual, news of our arrival has preceded us, and, not for the first time, we are greeted by people whose lives have been touched by the Lord. In particular, a woman who met my son right at this very spot.

"You are most welcome in my town," she tells us, focusing her attention on Mary, the leader of our group. "I have heard news that our Lord was put to death in Jerusalem but that three days later he rose from the dead. Tell me, is this true?"

Mary smiles and nods. "It is true. We are on our way to meet up with him again in Jerusalem."

"Come, then," the woman urges. "Stay in my home, and then I will go with you in the morning."

Once again we have comfortable lodgings and the best food imaginable. It is as if this trip has been planned from on high.

"I am afraid I may be getting spoiled," I admit to Sarah as we prepare for bed. "What if I get used to being treated like a queen?"

She laughs. "You, Mary? I do not think so. You seem to thrive on cooking and gardening and serving others. I do not think you shall ever be spoiled, my dear."

But I am unaccustomed to so much attention and so much preferential treatment, as if having given birth to the Son of God was something of my own doing. I try to explain again and again that I was simply the handmaid of God and, more importantly, I am now just another disciple to our Lord. But people do not seem to understand this. Or maybe they just do not care to accept it.

People seem determined that my being the mother of Jesus entitles me to special treatment. So much so that I actually begin to long for my hometown in Nazareth, where people not only refuse to acknowledge me as anything other than "that Mary" but often tend to put me down as well. Of course, I cannot admit as much to anyone, for I am sure it might sound like grumbling. And that is not how I mean it. I suppose it is only that, in my heart, I am still just an ordinary girl who likes to putter around barefoot in her garden and bounce children on her knee.

Although, I am surprised by something that happens in the night. I have slept in so many strange beds these past weeks that I sometimes wake up and cannot remember where I am. Such is the case tonight. As realization sinks in and I remember that I am in a home about a day's journey from Jerusalem, I sit here pondering over how much has happened. Then suddenly I remember my son's words that day when we met on the street during Passover. I remember how he had said, "It was your pure heart . . . the reason my Father chose you." And, well, I must admit that I do feel a bit special right now.

The next morning we are on our way to Jerusalem and, like little children with great expectations, there is much laughter and joy in the air. Our numbers have increased to nearly a hundred now, with more, like my own James, coming in the next day or two. Naturally, the others will have to find their own lodgings.

"Some of us will be staying in Bethany," Mary announces to the group when Jerusalem is clearly in sight and it is time to part ways. "But we will all meet in Jerusalem when the time is right." Then she makes a list of where our friends will be so that messengers can be sent to inform them of where we shall eventually gather. We part ways, returning to the original group of women who left from Magdala nearly two weeks ago.

It is a short journey on to Bethany, but I feel tired when we arrive. Martha comes out the door to greet us while we are still outside of her lovely home.

"You are weary, Mary," she says to me as she takes my arm and leads me up into her house. "Come and see your room, rest until suppertime, and then we will talk."

For the first time I am actually thankful for this kind of attention. For it is true, I am weary. But at least we are here now. And I know that with good rest among good friends, I will be ready for whatever is to happen next. I only hope it will involve my Lord. For, oh, how my heart aches to see him one more time!

20

"It seems impossible that it has been forty days since the Son of Man rose from the dead," Mary of Magdala says.

"How quickly it is passed," Martha agrees as a servant fills our wine cups.

"Yet so much has happened," Susanna says.

It is our first evening in Bethany, and we are gathered at Mary and Martha's fine dinner table. There are many beautiful cushions for us to recline upon. Some have fabric of embroidered silk. Numerous lovely serving dishes grace the table. The wine decanter looks as if it could be gold. But then I am no expert in such things.

Lazarus has gone somewhere with the men this evening, but there is a feeling of enthusiasm and hopeful anticipation among the women. Sounds of happy conversation and feminine laughter fill the air like musical instruments that are tuning up for an important performance. I am impressed with how well my sister Sarah fits in with these women of influence. This is probably because she was married to a prosperous merchant and is much more comfortable with material wealth than I shall ever be. But I am pleased to see her interacting with these lovely women with such ease. And I can see they like Jesus's aunt.

As usual, the food and service is much too fine for me, but, as usual, I keep these thoughts to myself. More and more I think I am a very plain woman with very plain tastes and simple needs. Even so, I tell myself to remember these times. Such memories will provide me with much amusement when I am back in my humble home, dining on bread and cucumbers for my supper.

Although I rested before dinner, I still

feel tired, and I excuse myself early and turn in before the others. It has not escaped my attention that I am among the oldest of this group of women. And, until now, I thought I managed to keep up rather well. But then I am of hardworking peasant stock, the kind of people who can toil in the fields for long hours without breaks. I should be able to keep up. But tonight I am as weary as a stone and hope to sleep just as soundly.

The next day there is excitement in the air. The disciples have returned after being with Jesus, and their faces are alight with joy. John takes me aside and describes what has happened. "It was wonderful, Mother," he begins. "He took us to the mountain with him, and once we were there he began to speak."

"What did he say?" I ask, hungry for more words of life.

"First he reminded us of how he once said that John baptized with water but that he would baptize with fire."

"Yes, I remember those words, but I never understood their meaning."

"The Lord said it would not be many days from now."

"That is why he has called us here to meet with him?" I ask, once again hoping I will still have the chance to see my Lord with my own eyes.

"Yes. After Jesus told us that, one of the men asked him if he would restore the kingdom of Israel now."

I nod. This does not surprise me. "What did the Lord say?"

"He said it is not for us to know these things. He said they are in the Father's timing and his authority."

"Yes. That sounds right."

"He also said that after the Holy Spirit comes we will all be empowered to be his witnesses, starting in Jerusalem, then throughout Judea and Samaria, and finally to the ends of the earth."

"The ends of the earth." I marvel at this. That sounds much bigger than just our nation of Israel.

"But then the most startling thing happened, Mother," John continues. "Jesus was standing on the ground, right in our midst, and then he began to lift up, straight up into the sky."

"Oh my!"

"And we all just stood there gaping at him. Some of us had our mouths hanging wide open. Then our Lord called down to us and said, 'Why are you looking into the sky like that? For it is the same way I go into heaven now that I will come back to you one day.' "

"Does that mean he is gone?" I ask, feeling dismayed by this possibility.

"I do not know for sure."

"Of course," I tell him. "How could you? Only the Father knows these things."

While John's news is truly wonderful, I still feel a bit disappointed that I have not yet seen the Lord. I know that I am only a poor woman from Nazareth and that the Lord has much more important affairs to tend to than someone as insignificant as me. But I secretly long to see him just the same. Only now, after hearing how he was lifted up into the heavens, well, I am afraid that perhaps he has left us for good. Still, I remind myself that this is not for me to concern myself with. The Lord knows what he is doing. All I must do is trust him. And I believe I can do that.

By the next day the men have located a large upper-story room where all of us will gather to wait for his coming. We are full of excitement and great expectation as we prepare to go and join them there. Some of the disciples say Jesus is not going to come to this place himself but that he is simply going to send his helper—the Holy Spirit—that we may be empowered to be his ministers. Others still believe that Jesus is coming again. I find it somewhat amusing that even now, after all we have seen and heard, his disciples still cannot seem to agree on much. Well, other than that Jesus is the Son of God. I suppose that is enough.

I go with the women into Jerusalem, and soon we find the right place and climb up the stairs until we reach the upper story. It is a spacious room with columns and high ceilings, but it quickly fills with dozens of Jesus's followers. During our first day we are all very enthused, watching and waiting and expecting a miracle. My zeal is slightly dampened by the fact that none of my children from Nazareth have arrived yet. I am concerned that James may have changed his mind, or perhaps he will not get here in time.

I slip off to a corner in the back of the room, and there I bow my head and pray. "Dear Lord," I whisper, "I beg you, please, ensure that your brother James, and perhaps some of your other relatives, are able to get here soon, and in time so that they too might see you and receive your Holy Spirit. Amen."

I continue this prayer and others like it several times into the night and during the following two days, feeling a mixture of relief and impatience, as we all continue to wait and wait and wait. Then, just before sundown of the third day, my sons arrive. Not only James, but Joses and Simon and Judas have come as well! I run to greet them and hug each of them to my heart, thanking Jehovah for bringing them to us.

Then I take these men straight to John, introducing them as if they are all related as brothers. Fortunately, my own sons do not seem offended by this. John takes them around the room and introduces them to the other ten disciples. It is not long before my sons are gathered around Simon Peter and John, listening to these two dear men retelling some of the things they have seen and heard during these past three years, and especially lately. The other disciples inject bits and pieces here and there, and in the course of the next few days, my four sons are being thoroughly educated into their half brother's incredible ministry.

Day turns into night turns into day, and yet we continue to wait. How long will it take? I must admit that I even feel brief gusts of doubt. What if Jesus's disciples did not hear him quite right? Or what if we are in the wrong place? I know this is foolishness, but it is only because I am so tired of waiting. I feel that I have been waiting my whole life. Still, I sit in my corner and try to remain faithful. Waiting, waiting, waiting . . .

How long must we wait, Lord? We have been up here in this room for more than a week now. I think it is ten days altogether. In some ways it reminds me of that other time of waiting. Certainly, that was a much darker time, a more hopeless time, and only three days. Even so, this is beginning to feel like eternity to me. I sit quietly in my corner in the back of the room, where I have remained most of the time, as we continue to wait. All of our needs have been graciously seen to by servants that Martha of Bethany and Mary of Magdala have made arrangements for. Food and water is carried up. We have bedding to sleep on. And here we have stayed day after day.

I realize during this confinement that I am unaccustomed to being indoors for such extended periods. I am a woman who needs the blue sky overhead and the dusty earth beneath my feet. But, other than to tend to my body's most basic needs, I refuse to leave this stuffy room for long. I am too worried that I might miss him while I am out. And I could not bear to miss him again.

I tell no one of this, but I have grown weary, very weary, during these past two days. I am weary from travel, weary from waiting, weary with this earthly life altogether. I am beginning to think I am a very old woman, too old for such things. Perhaps it is time for me to go home to Nazareth and then to lay my body down next to my dear Joseph, beneath the ground. That is how weary I am right now. But I sense that I am not the only one. The room has been heavy with quietness today. I think everyone is weary of waiting.

Suddenly there is a change. I think we all feel it, for it seems that instantly and simultaneously everyone comes to attention. Some rise to their feet, and I discover that I too am standing, although I do not recall getting up. And then a blast of wind bursts into the room, almost like a whirlwind or a small tornado, although that seems impossible. With the howling of the wind in my ears, and with dust and debris and something else—is it light?—whirling around, it seems that everyone in the room has disappeared—or are they obscured?—except for me, and I feel that I stand all alone with this loud rushing in my ears, and a feeling of energy—or is it fire?—surges through my head clear down to my toes! It is unlike anything I have ever experienced! And yet it is familiar. In some ways it is like that night so long ago when God's Spirit came upon me and I conceived his son. But so much more so!

I stand with my hands and face lifted to the heavens, worshiping God, fully expecting to be lifted and swept away with this wind. I am hoping I will be taken up in the same manner that my Lord has gone before me. And then, as suddenly as it began, it is over.

I look around and am surprised to see that everyone else is still here. But I know that nothing will ever be the same. Their faces look as astonished as I feel. But there is something more—each face has an expression of pure ecstasy—as if they have looked into the soul of God. Indeed, that is how I feel.

Before long some of the disciples and others are beginning to speak in foreign languages, and many other astounding things are happening, and miracles too. It is wonderful and incredible, and yet I have this strong sense that it is time for me to go. It is not a negative feeling, not as if I want to leave these people I love so dearly, but simply a knowledge within me—maybe it is the Holy Spirit, the Helper. But somehow I know deep inside that it is time for me to leave.

With so much activity and excitement in this room, no one notices as I slip out the back door and head down into the street below. I walk quietly with my head slightly bowed as I consider the amazing thing that has just happened to me. My heart is so full! Full to the point of overflowing. And I realize now that I no longer need to see the Lord with my own eyes. I realize that he, by the power of his Holy Spirit, is living inside me now. I do not know how, but somehow I know this without doubt. Just as assuredly as I knew that the Son of God lived within my womb more than thirty-three years ago, I know that the Son of God lives here now. Only more so.

I head for the city gates, thinking I will first go to the house in Bethany, where I will gather my things, and then I will pre- pare to leave. Just as I am outside of the city, I notice someone is walking beside me. An old man, I think, for his gait is slow and smooth, but I continue to walk, keeping my head down as I ponder all these things and make my plans.

"Where are you going?" the stranger asks.

Surprised that he is addressing me, I glance at him, then simply say, "I am going to Nazareth."

"Why are you going to Nazareth?" he asks.

Unsure of the answer, I reach up and touch my little secret seed pocket, checking to see if my seed is still there. "To plant seeds," I tell the man, as if that should make sense.

"Is that all?" he asks.

Suddenly I wonder why this man is so curious about me, but I answer him anyway. "And then I am going to harvest."

I am sure this stranger must think I am crazy if I plan to harvest when it is still springtime. So I turn and study his face to determine if he is confused by my answer. But he just smiles.

And that is when I know. He is no stranger. But before I can say anything, before I can fall upon my knees and thank him and worship him, he is gone. In a glorious flash of pure golden light, he vanishes. But his smile remains with me. Such a smile. And that is not all. He remains with me as well, and I know that wherever he leads, that is where I will go. But right now he is leading me back to Nazareth to plant seeds and then to harvest.

The Beginning

Melody Carlson is the prolific author of more than a hundred books, including fiction, nonfiction, and gift books for adults, young adults, and children. Her most recent novels are *Finding Alice* and *Crystal Lies* (WaterBrook). Her writing has won several awards, including a Gold Medallion for *King of the Stable* (Crossway, 1998) and a Romance Writers of America Rita Award for *Homeward* (Multnomah, 1997). She lives with her husband in Sisters, Oregon.